HOW TO THRIVE
IN AN ECONOMIC DISASTER

HOW TO
THRIVE
IN AN ECONOMIC
DISASTER

Jimmy Yamada, Jr.

WHITE
MOUNTAIN
CASTLE
PUBLISHING, LLC

www.whitemountaincastle.com
Kapolei, Hawai'i

HOW TO THRIVE
IN AN ECONOMIC DISASTER

Copyright © 2015 Jimmy Yamada, Jr.
Published by White Mountain Castle Publishing, LLC

WHITE
MOUNTAIN
CASTLE
PUBLISHING, LLC

White Mountain Castle Publishing, LLC
P.O. Box 700833
Kapolei, Hawaii 96709

Email: whitemountaincastle@yahoo.com
Website: whitemountaincastle.com

Unless otherwise noted,
Scripture is taken from the HOLY BIBLE, NEW INTERNATIONAL VERSION, Copyright © 1973, 1978, 1984 by International Bible Society. Used by permission of Zondervan Publishing House.
All rights reserved.

Cover Design & Text Formatting by Sherrie Dodo
Cover Photos by ©iStockphoto.com
Back Cover Photo by Marc Schecther

ISBN 978-0-9815219-9-2

Printed in Korea

This book is dedicated to my wife, Diana.
She helped me thrive and get through my
economic disasters.
She was the rock of my life before I
found the true ROCK.
She solidly stood by me when I didn't have a
clear path to my future.

Now our paths are united, our family is
Thriving and is solidly connected to the
ROCK, who is Jesus Christ.

Thank you Diana, you are the
"Love of my life."

TABLE OF CONTENTS

INTRODUCTION

ARE CHRISTIANS PREPARED?

Christians who live in America and love God, trust Him, and have great faith may actually be ill prepared if an economic disaster hits. The early Christians had great faith, yet economic calamities affected them as well. Many Christians believe they will be exempt from hardship, but this is not biblical; God will walk with us through disaster. The early Christians' faith was not negatively affected by economic calamities, and Christianity grew. American Christians are relatively wealthy compared to the rest of the world and have grown accustomed to the wealth that God provides. The safety net that government has provided for us through its various programs as well as protective bailouts is another reason why we (myself included) are not ready for an economic disaster.

We may think we are living out our great faith and trust God, but we are blindsided and unprepared when a severe recession or depression hits suddenly. I know I struggle in times of difficulty, when things go wrong and think, "Self, I am struggling for God's sake, and God will provide." I call this faith, but inside I really hope God will deliver me from my lack of planning, saving, risk-taking, and general unpreparedness.

I am writing this to help me think through an economic disaster. I bring God into my journey through my past, my present, and try to plan for how I might thrive if one hits in the future. I do not have the answer, but I am on a journey to discover how God's hand was with me through the lives of my parents and my wife Diana, as well as my family. This may help me recognize how He is with me today, guiding me. More importantly, I am trying to discover how He would have me live and thrive as the future unfolds. All futures are uncertain, but I think the current future is more uncertain than ever before.

JOIN ME IN MY JOURNEY

For those who have difficulty when minor challenges occur, I invite you to walk with me. This could apply to moms and dads, businessmen and women, executives, workingmen, and the retired or soon-to-retire families. The main focus of this book will be how we walk with our families. I once believed that if I could thrive with my family in difficult situations, I could get through anything life throws at me. So that was my ultimate goal. In the past, I know that my dysfunction caused me to react unpleasantly in times of great pressure, even towards my family. So I think thriving cannot be my target. It's like happiness. You cannot aim for it, for you will seek pleasure to gain happiness. Seeking pleasure, while aiming for happiness is a sure way to crash and burn. Aim for Jesus, get joy as a by-product, and you will thrive.

I try to lay out a practical as well as Biblical foundation why an economic disaster may lie ahead and the potential nature of that disaster. I do not deal with other disasters but the principles learned may well help us stand strong in the faith.

If you are not a believer, this book may also be for you as the principles involved may help you maneuver through your own calamities. My thoughts on the economic models come from men that appear to have wisdom from God. I have gleaned from them and share with you. Use what you can from what I share.

This book is not predicting an economic disaster, but deals with how we can be prepared if one strikes, like during the 2008-2009 period. I do, however, build a case that an economic disaster is possible, and more importantly, why many may be blindsided.

GOD'S GUIDING HAND

I draw lessons from my past family life and see how God prepared my family and me. I know he has prepared you also. I look back at my past and recognize how God showed up in my past, which I call "God's hand." I will also look at the signs of the times that seem to point to an economic disaster waiting to unfold. I try to point out how believers can actually thrive during an economic disaster and in any type of disaster. "Is Jesus enough?" is the all-important question. The question may seem trite in times of disaster so I try to explore how I might get to the point where Jesus is enough.

I look back at my family's past to demonstrate how God used pain and suffering in their lives to develop strength of character in them. I see that God was there for them and was walking with them, even if He wasn't yet living in them (John 14:17). I believe everyone has similar pain and suffering in their lives, but what may be missing is the recognition of "God with us." God was always there with us. God was always working "for our good." If we recognize that, we can trust that He will always be there. The Apostle Paul taught that he suffered a lot and wanted to die, but those things happened that he might rely on God (2 Corinthians 1). I believe the ultimate ability to thrive in any disaster is to rely on God to become the fruitful person He desires. This cannot happen unless we continually practice reliance on Him. As I look back, I realize that as I walked on the

X

journey with my family, friends, and workers, the journey enabled me to practice my faith.

GOD'S ULTIMATE GOOD: BECOME LIKE JESUS

I lay out a plan to reach my goal, which I believe is God's ultimate desire for me, and maybe for you, too. My plan states certain theological truths. They may not be the ultimate theological truths, but these are truths that have been effective in my aim for who God wants me to become. Following this plan may help me reach my objective, which will be to thrive in all circumstances, including an economic disaster, which I believe is currently unfolding. However, that disaster is only a prelude to God's ultimate disaster, or ultimate blessing, depending on your view of the world.

I believe that God's ultimate desire is for me to be conformed to the image of Christ, or to become like Jesus (Romans 8:29). He is working towards that end for you and me. In order to get us there, he puts in our hearts and souls a mission and a cause to make a difference in the world for the sake of His Name. Whoever of us discovers his/her mission will continue to walk in that as his/her ultimate cause because he/she will know it is God's assignment for him/her. In that mission, God will walk with us, carry us, enlighten us, empower us, and will never leave us. As we walk, He molds us to become like Jesus, and we stay connected to Jesus through the Holy Spirit. As we become like Jesus, we become fruitful (Galatians 5:22) and are able to thrive in all circumstances.

We can thrive because we know He loves us, and we can never disappoint Him. He becomes our ultimate audience. Our family and friends help us along the way, but often they can distract us and send us the wrong signals. They are a crucial part of God working for our good, but they cannot be the reason we live. Although our family and friends are part of the hundredfold blessing of God, they can not be our ultimate mission. My family and friends are the base from which I operate and are essential to growth, but the ultimate desire of God is that through all circumstances, work, ministry, and mission, I become like Christ.

We never give up in the face of great suffering and disappointment, because we always have hope. Our blessed hope is our relationship with Jesus, but we also have hope in knowing that God cannot fail in His endeavor to help us become like Jesus. We can fail only if we quit and stop walking. Some may think they fail because the mission or task at hand seems impossible, but they are focusing on the wrong mountain. The mission or the cause that God births in us is not the mountain that we are climbing. To become like Jesus is the mountain, for this is God's ultimate desire for us.

God created us in his image, and after man's fall, God had a plan to restore us to the image that we were created to be. Jesus was the plan. God cannot fail. We are predestined to become like Jesus. Unfortunately, the process is slow. It is in that slowness that He can do His great work in us as long as we don't give up.

GOD WORKS IT OUT SO WE GET THERE

The underlying theme throughout the book is Romans 8:28, "And we know that God causes all things to work together for good to those who love God, to those who are called according to His purpose" (NASB). I've always looked at this as God causing all the situations for all the people in my life to work together for *my* good. I am not any more special to God than anyone else. To God, everyone is special. However, since I look at life from my perspective, my paradigm is to see how God worked things out especially for me. If my wife Diana was writing this book, she could write how God humbled me, developed me, and blessed me, and then used me as He worked all things together for her good.

So is Paul writing about my good or Diana's good? Whatever is good for me, must be good for her; and whatever is good for her, must be good for me. Right? Of course! Paul continues in Romans 8:29, "For God knew his people in advance, and he chose them to become like his son" (NLT). Can it be that simple that the ultimate goal that God desires is that we become like Jesus? So is God working all things out so we become like Jesus, and as we do, is God working His ultimate good for us? The answer to this simple truth may be the key to thriving.

One of the things I've noticed is that God continuously does His good work throughout the world in everyday life, through people's lives, through believers and non-believers, in all areas of life. He works through our churches, our families, our workplaces, our businesses, our government, our leaders, our social programs, our laws and our legal system. He permeates all areas of our lives and is ubiquitous. He can have the rocks cry out, and He can use donkeys (Numbers 22). I believe He leaves traces of His working in patterns we see in life. These patterns are obvious if we are looking for them. There is a pattern to God's hand working good for all people. The amazing thing is that He uses us as part of His pattern.

I try to point out the patterns that I've been able to see in my life, and I hope that you can look back, see the patterns in your life, and be enriched and encouraged knowing that He was there, always working good for you. I pray that He increases your faith as you come to recognize that He will always be "causing all things to work" for your ultimate good. This extends to our immediate families and all people with whom He connects us.

GOD'S COMMAND: BE FRUITFUL

God told Adam, to "be fruitful" (Genesis 1:28, Galatians 5:22). I believe that in order to know that we thrive in difficult situations, there has to be evidence of fruitfulness. During the World Trade Center disaster, there was a lot of fruit (love, joy, kindness, etc.) in the actions of many who helped others. Webster defines the word thrive as "to grow vigorously, to gain in wealth and possessions, to progress toward or realize a goal despite or because of circumstances."[1] For the believers, thriving must be seen from God's view. Therefore, we grow vigorously in our agape love for God through Jesus and through dependence on the Holy Spirit. Our wealth is in our relationship with God through Jesus, activated by the Holy Spirit, but our relationship with God is only measureable in our love touch for others.

We know we're becoming fruitful when we can walk through a distress or disaster and be more concerned for others than for ourselves. Our initial thoughts should be "How can I help them? What do they need?" Fruitfulness cannot be hiding in my closet, not coming out until the disaster is over, and claiming, "I was at peace in my closet with Jesus." Fruitfulness is fully engaging in the disaster and doing what you believe the Lord would want you to do. What if you and I are part of God's plan of working good for others? If I am part of God's plan, then in any situation, even normal ones, I need to be thinking that God wants me to react in a certain way so He can work out good for someone. In other words, it's really not only for my good, but for others as well. Do I know what He wants me to do? For our spouses, oftentimes, God wants us to do nothing.

I've come to realize that my family, my financial and economic blessings are related to my ability to thrive and be fruitful. I ponder, "If I lost everything like Job (Book of Job): my family, my home, my business, my health, and all my wealth, would I still be fruitful and be able to thrive?" If I am honest, I think not. So this book is mainly for me to help me thrive. Some can ponder life with God and come away with instant revelation and be truly "all in" very easily. For me, it's not that easy or quick. Maybe it's because I have a lifetime (45 years as an atheist) of bad habits to overcome. Maybe I'm slow. Maybe my brain gets in the way because I'm a thinker, and thinkers don't do well in hot water. They think and plan a strategy of what to do. Diana is a doer. When she is in hot water, she just jumps and moves. I think she could thrive better in a disaster because she is a doer.

Maybe God blessed me with too much. I know that to equate being fruitful and thriving with my wealth and the goods that God has blessed me with is foolish. I confess that I am foolish.

GOD'S DESIRE: RICH AND POOR TOGETHER?

In America, we have two groups of people: those who have "enough" (the rich and the middle class, even if they are struggling today) and the poor (who I'll define as those living below the poverty level). What if both groups are missing the focus of life? What if those who have enough equate thriving to having all the trappings of having "enough?" What if the poor think they cannot thrive because they don't have "enough?" What if God desires that the "enough" group realizes His ultimate truth that Jesus is actually enough for life and fruitfulness? What if God desires that those in the "not enough" group realize that they don't need more stuff and provision but they can thrive if they also realize that Jesus is enough for life and fruit-fulness? What if, as Ed Silvoso suggests, both groups have what the other group needs, and only in loving each other will both groups be able to thrive? What if God is orchestrating for both groups to come together to help one another and reach the unity He so desires? If He is working, what would that look like?

IS GOD ENOUGH?

One of the biblical truths in the Bible is Jesus is enough (2 Peter 1:3, John 1:4). Since we all may be a little off-course (you may be more on-course than me), Paul tells us that God will "cause all things to work together" so we get on course and are fruitful and thrive.

I believe that it's possible that He could use an economic disaster, or any of life's disasters, to help both rich and poor realize the true meaning of being fruitful. The group that has enough now might lose much of what they have and become poor. The families would be forced to depend on each other, which happens in times of calamity. Then in working together as a family unit, they may find that Jesus is truly enough. The poor might not be too greatly impacted by an economic disaster: they already don't have much physical wealth, but since they are rich in faith, they may actually teach the "enough" group how to live with Jesus as enough.

Job went through his disaster, and at the end God blessed him. But what if the ultimate blessing wasn't the doubling of wealth that God gave him, but the encounter with God that He had in Job 38-40? What if the only way to reach a truly rich encounter with God was through his trials, sufferings and pain? What if the ultimate life experience is one where Jesus is enough, and by going through life, you become like Jesus? Then no matter what you went through, you would thrive. Wouldn't that be wonderful? I know that I am not there, and it's easier to write about these things than live them.

I'M ON A JOURNEY

I take a journey trying to get a handle on some of these thoughts. I journey through my past and attempt to see God's hand in my family's past and hope to discover that He is enough. As I gain confidence that I am on my journey with God, I hope to understand His plan for me. Maybe I will discover that as I walk through life, God will cause me to become more like Jesus. What would that look like? Maybe my life will not look like what I initially wanted with blessings, favor, signs and wonders, and accolades from my family. Funny, I always wanted to impress Diana. Maybe I didn't have to. Maybe she always loved me regardless. What if becoming like Jesus allows me just to enjoy Diana, the way she is without trying to impress her. What if becoming like Jesus allowed me to automatically go to our Lord in all tough situations? Could it be that simple?

I invite you to journey with me, and maybe you will move a step in the same direction and also get a clearer picture of His plan for you. If you glean some good insights, then all glory goes to God. My theology tells me that only the Holy Spirit gives revelation: He can use a donkey or this book.

THE JOURNEY DESCRIBED

Chapter 1 describes the potential economic disaster unfolding. I hope to help you become aware so you are not blind-sided. There are things you may be able to do now to prepare yourself, your family and your businesses.

Chapter 2 lays out a biblical backdrop for an economic disaster. The Bible lays out a case for the return of Jesus Christ and economic disaster near the time of that event. I believe that we are very close, but remember God's time is different from ours. "...With the Lord one day is like a thousand years, and a thousand years like one day" (2 Peter 3:8, NASB).

Chapter 3 presents the concept that part of God causing all things to work together for our good is that He works good in our family tree. God could use what may seem like suffering to us for our good. We might be able to understand and see things from God's perspective and see that God's Hand was always there.

Chapter 4 focuses on how God developed me all my life so that I can be a person that He can use. His work of conforming me to be ready for His purpose started long before I was saved. God doesn't waste time or people. God doesn't miss an opportunity to start changing our attitudes, our minds, and hearts. He doesn't sit around waiting for us to accept His salvation before He starts working in us.

Chapter 5 focuses on God guiding me to my mission and clarifying my mission. I now recognize that all of my life was preparation for this season, and this season is preparation for the next season. God will not be limited by our limited vision.

Chapter 6 focuses on God and my business mission. God works in all areas of life. In God's kingdom, there is no separation between the Christian world and the secular world. God controls the universe with His word. We see His ultimate control in atoms, in the animal and plant kingdoms, as well as in people's cultures. God is ubiquitous, and His Hand can be seen clearly if we can recognize the patterns through which He works. The secular world tries very hard to disconnect the world from God's control and influence, so they give God secular names like "Mother Nature." God is really the one in control.

Chapter 7 focuses on how we can thrive and be fruitful by becoming like Jesus. I highlight the power of the family as the most powerful mission field to help our kids and our husbands and wives also to become like Jesus. I close with the story of Dietrich Bonhoeffer who was a man who became like Jesus, and I draw conclusions from his life and beliefs.

I know I am far from where God wants me to be, but I know I want what God wants for me. I trust He will accomplish His good work in me as I walk with Him. I don't profess to have the answers, but I hope to discover some as I take this journey. Maybe as I realign my heart, mind and soul to God's way of life, I hope to reach a life of thriving no matter what lies ahead.

1

BE READY BY SEEING
THE SIGN OF THE TIMES:
THRIVING THROUGH AWARENESS

SOMETHING'S OUT THERE

Anyone with eyes and ears can look around, and sense that something is drastically wrong with the economy, be it locally, nationally, or worldwide. We have so much information coming to us that we can be desensitized to reality and truth. As Pontus Pilate asked, "What is truth?" No one can really know the underlying true situation in the world economy.

We live in a world where the powers that make the decisions seem to be clueless to solutions. They know the world struggles with many problems and issues, but no one seems to have a clear plan for the problems that plague us. Is it possible that the world issues have gotten so complex that there is no solution without intense pain? The powers in control dislike pain so they seem to allow themselves to be carried along as if they were floating down a river. They are not aware that a dangerous waterfall may lie at the end of the river.

Let's look at a few of the issues at hand.

UNITED STATES ISSUES

1. United States total Government debt is officially over $17 trillion. Total US debt is over $50 trillion.

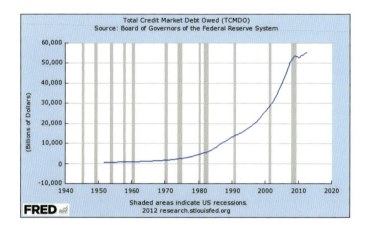

2. Total US unfunded liabilities for social programs (Medicare, Welfare, Social Security, Retirement) may be over $100 trillion.

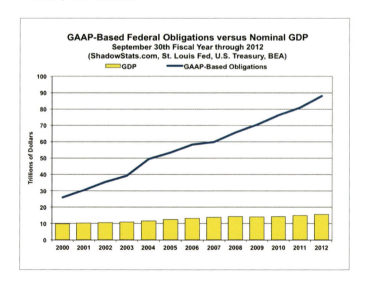

3. The number of people unemployed in the US is 23 million or more, depending on how the total is counted.

4. 47 million people in the US receive food stamps.

5. 127 million people in the US receive some form of government assistance, including 61 million who receive Social Security and Medicare and 66 million who receive other types of assistance, such as welfare, food stamps, housing credits, Medicaid, etc.

6. The US dollar has fallen 35% in 10 years and 90% in 50 years.

7. Drought conditions exist across the United States.

8. The number of violent mass shootings shows something is drastically wrong.

9. US defense expenditures of $711 billion in 2012 are more than the combined total defense budgets of the next 10 largest national defense budgets combined.

EUROPE ISSUES

1. Will the Euro fall apart?

2. Will the European common market fall apart?

3. Is there a limit to United States and German support for the Euro?

4. Can European government debt ever be paid?

WORLD

1. 925 million people were malnourished in 2011. Food shortages in developed nations can cause extreme stress in those nations.

2. According to the Bank of International Settlements, total derivatives outstanding are valued at $700 trillion. Others estimate that the number is as high as $1,500 trillion ($1.5 quadrillion). If you don't know what a derivative is, that is all right because no one really understands them.

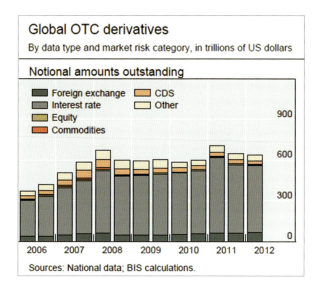

3. There are wars all over the world, some big and some small.

Some of these issues and numbers are meaningless to you and me. We read about them in the news. They don't seem like they can affect us as we go about our daily lives. No one can truly know how these global issues and conflicts will ultimately affect us until something hits. We cannot see it, nor can we understand it, but these issues will impact us some time down the road. The problems can be compared to cancer. Can you see cancer? Most normal medical checkups will not detect pancreatic cancer until the cancer has developed, and by then, it's too late.

Although the underlying issue in the world is a spiritual one, eventual breakdown is apparent in the world's political, business, fiscal, and monetary policies, and in its social unrest.

CAN THIS AFFECT ME?

While no one can see tomorrow's disaster today, we can prepare for a worst-case storm before the storm comes. Lest you think, "Why prepare? The storm will never come," I believe that even if an economic disaster has only a small probability today, if we extend the period to three to five years, the probabilities increase dramatically.

God tells us that he is always working out good in our lives, preparing us all of our lives, so you can sit at peace today quietly reading this book. The Bible teaches that suffering is good for our development as it develops patience, character, hope and love (Romans 5:3-5). So it is possible that God allows or orchestrates tough situations in our lives so we can grow spiritually and emotionally so that we may be fruitful for Him.

As I look back in the lives of my dad, my mom, and my wife Diana, I can see God allowing challenges, orchestrating situations, and protecting my loved ones so they would become strong and tough. This helps them later in life, especially as it pertains to me.

I can see that He was there for the Yamadas and know that He was there for you. His Word tells us that. You may not have seen Him, but He was with you. As you understand how He operates, then you can look back for His hand in your past, and you will see His hand working for your good.

BELIEVERS SHOULD ALWAYS BE PREPARED

I will be using the term believers for Christians throughout this book, "believers" meaning believers in the Lord Jesus Christ. Although this book is written for believers, the principals, concepts and practices will be helpful to those who are not believers, so that they can also be prepared.

The Bible is our instruction manual for surviving and thriving in any type of disaster. However, the main focus for this book will be an economic disaster that could affect you and your family if any one of the following economic disasters occurred.

1. World stock markets could crash.
2. World bond markets could crash, and long-term bond rates could hit double digits.

3. Banking systems of the world could default.
4. US unemployment could skyrocket.
5. US government debt could hit $20 trillion. US government deficit could hit $2 trillion per year.
6. The US dollar could lose its standing as the world's reserve currency.
7. US inflation could return to double digits.
8. Food shortages in developed nations, including the US, could result in rioting in the streets.
9. US Gross Domestic Product (GDP) could fall for a long period of time, as it did in Japan.
10. Germany could decide to stop supporting the European Common Market and the Euro.

Any one of these issues could trigger something very bad in the business you own or for which you work, your investments, your retirement income, your family, and, in effect, your way of life. Believers might think, "Well I'll depend on God then," which is very well said but not easily lived out.

My challenge to you is to start depending on God now, and be ready if something bad hits. Dietrich Bonhoeffer said, "Only the believer is obedient, and only he who obeys believes."[1]

Now all believers obey God in some ways, but very few believers obey God in all ways. Some may say that is impossible. While that is true this side of heaven, Jesus told us to strive for it, to be perfect. My focus in this book is to present a few perfect target principles from the Bible that may help me move closer to God's model for surviving and thriving if an economic disaster hits. If you receive a benefit, that's great.

ARE BELIEVERS MUCH DIFFERENT?

Believers should live differently from secular American culture today. *Beasts of the Southern Wild* was a movie that impacted me deeply. The impact was not in its entertainment value, but it clarified the dysfunctional nature of souls who grow up in a secular culture. The movie was set in a Bayou community with a father named Wink and his daughter Hushpuppy who is six years old. They live in the "Bathtub." Hushpuppy's mother has already died, and she and her father each live in their own house. The houses are built behind a levee system, and during storms, the whole area floods, so their only means of transportation is a homemade boat fashioned from a truck.

Wink's whole life is wrapped up in raising Hushpuppy to be strong, but he is sick and doesn't want to let Hushpuppy see him die. A couple of scenes stand out. Hushpuppy tries to crack open a crab with a knife, but Wink stops her. He grabs the crab, breaks it with his hands, and then eats some. He tells Hushpuppy, "Beast it." Their *hanai* (adopted) family starts chanting, "Beast it, beast it," so that when Hushpuppy tears open the crab, cheers erupts. No one will ever change the way Hushpuppy eats crab.

In another scene, after the whole area is flooded, local officials come to rescue the remnants that refused to leave during the warnings to evacuate. They rescue the motley gang and take them to a shelter. Doctors realize Wink's condition is serious and that he will die if he doesn't receive surgery. Wink's only concern is for Hushpuppy because he doesn't want her to hear them talk about his death.

They eventually subdue him and do the worst thing imaginable for Wink: they plug him into the wall with tubes. Wink organizes an escape for the gang and eventually tells Hushpuppy he's going to die. He prefers to go home and die rather than stay, have an operation, and possibly live. The cultural upbringing in which Wink raises Hushpuppy is so powerful, and it helps me understand the difficult challenges ahead if people change their cultural habits. Ed Silvoso would say that these are strongholds that prevent them seeing the way Jesus sees. Only God can really accomplish true transformation, but it takes time, as it did for the Apostle Peter who was with the Lord daily for three years.

DO BELIEVERS REALLY REACT DIFFERENTLY?

Believers also have strongholds that prevent them from seeing the way Jesus sees. God changes us as new creations in Christ, but in certain areas, we are who we are, and change is slow. We want what we want, and the cultures in which we were raised make it difficult to change the way we see things.

We add on the name of Jesus to our prayers, almost like adding ingredients to a cooking recipe: we add new ingredients into whatever we already cook. I know that anything I do, even in spiritual disciplines, very easily becomes rote and routine. I know practice and self-control is important, but sometimes my body moves and my mouth moves, but my heart is left behind.

I desire Jesus to have complete control over my life because I know the Word tells me He should. However, spiritual change is slow, and my old habits are sticky. Maybe it's only me. I feel like Paul when he said, "What I want to do I do not do, but what I hate I do" (Romans 7:15). I get upset at certain situations, and I go back to my base evil nature. Hushpuppy would grow up believing that Wink taught her the right way and would live that life, always defaulting to her base nature in which she would "beast it."

Believers love family, often more than God. It's difficult to put God first because we grow up with this foundational belief in our souls (hearts, minds, emotions). We trust in Jesus for forgiveness for all our wrongs, but we still want what we want. How can loving family be bad? While there is nothing wrong with loving family, if we truly love God with all our heart, soul, mind and strength, then we would follow His way in how we live out our family love. How does this translate to living a life where God has priority over family? I hope to expand on this during my journey in this book.

People addicted to drugs and alcohol have a cultural history, disposition, and lifestyle that drives them to want what they want even if they get "saved." Some may argue that if they cannot stop their addiction, they are probably not saved. When I lose my file for my message that I've been working on for hours, for the most part, I passively sigh, or cry. But the other day, I found myself beasting it. "Damn, damn, damn," I cried, while pounding my fists on my table. I was only angry with myself. After a minute, I settled down and refocused. I realize there is always something that can trigger me, although I come back to God eventually. I rationalize and think, "I'm not hurting anyone," but I know I hurt God. I demonstrated a lack of trust.

I will not measure people's choices against their salvation as the measuring stick. I think many have difficulty depending on God during stressful and painful moments. My goal is to shorten the time between the climactic event and when I cry out to God saying, "Oh God, oh God, help me." Maybe then He might help me to become more like Jesus. Since that is what God desires for me, in the next ten years I might make some headway if I keep Jesus as the focus.

DO YOU HAVE A TRIGGER?

I believe each of us have a trigger that can cause us to lose it for a moment. While the believer can quickly regain focus, it is directly proportional to the measure of faith he has. Is Jesus enough? Are you being real?

In *Beasts of the Southern Wild*, Wink and Hushpuppy along with their friends lived all of their lives in the Bathtub. They found it impossible to embrace a new paradigm, and Wink preferred to die at home rather than live away from home. Their culture created a default way of looking at life. The disaster for them was not the storm and ensuing flood; the disaster was not even death. The disaster was being plugged into the wall. That was his trigger. For people from the Bathtub, the trigger was staying in a shelter away from their homes, not knowing how long they would be there. They would rather live in their homes in the Bathtub with eight feet of water all around them than live in a shelter without freedom to do as they pleased.

Believers have a trigger that can cause us to act differently from our underlying belief system. We prefer to live with all the pleasures of our earthly tents, our earthly possessions, our businesses, our kids, our pleasures and delights. Not that any of these are bad, but for those accustomed to them, if we ever fear losing some part of our kingdom or way of life, we plead with God to bless us, protect us, and let us keep what He gave us. If someone threatens our way of life, God help him. I know this is true for me, and although God is in the process of healing me from this selfishness, I am far from healed. Woe for you if you are like me.

One trigger that Americans have is their economic wealth. I won't bore you with statistics on how much better we are than the rest of the world. You already know that. We live in a rented apartment or own a condo or home, have tons of furniture and stuff, own one to three cars, have some retirement savings, own businesses, etc. What would happen if suddenly, you were at risk of losing every material thing you had? In the last economic downturn of 2008 to 2009 many were put in this position. Even more came close. If you weren't concerned, you may have been like the man who fell off a two-hundred-story building who said as he fell, "So far, so good." Some of us were oblivious to how close the financial system came to a collapse. It didn't happen because the governments of the world went "all in."

ALL IN, TEXAS HOLD'EM STYLE

Over the past sixty years, the world has experienced an economic boom like none ever seen before in history. Over the past twenty years, the powerful economists in control of the economic system have embraced a new philosophy. It really is more of the same, but there is a small twist, which I'll explain.

Keynesian economists believe that by adjusting the system, the economists in control can minimize the level of pain for those in America. (I'll focus on America, although this is true across the world). All they have to do is pour money into whatever needs fixing. The following are examples of situations where money was used as a quick fix.

- The stock market crash of 1987
- The 1998 Russian default and Long-Term Capital Management debacle
- The dot-com NASDAQ crash
- The market crash following the 9/11 attack

- The subprime mortgage crisis and market crash
- The European nations default trouble

Note the increasing level of commitment by the powers in control. After the failure of Long-Term Capital Management in 1998 (if you never heard of this, it was because the powers in control were successful), in order to prevent pain, poured money into the system, which created the dot-com bubble.

After the dot-com bubble burst, the powers in control poured money to save the NASDAQ and small capital stock market, and thus saved a larger group from the pain that would have occurred.

The 9/11 attacks created a panic and a larger stock market crash, and to save the stock market and prevent pain, the powers in control poured greater amounts of money into the system, which led to the real estate bubble.

The real estate bubble led to trouble in the banking system. The powers in control poured ever-increasing amounts of money into the system and changed the rules of the game when they realized they didn't have enough money. Essentially, the whole banking system was holding bad Level 3 paper. The Financial Accounting Standards Board rules required revaluing that paper, forcing institutions to write down Level 3 assets. Taking haircuts a few firms failed, including Bear Stearns and Lehman.

Some of the powers in control realized that if everyone wrote down their Level 3 assets, the banking system would be in jeopardy. In Hawaiian pidgin, the banking system would be "busted." So to be sure that no one would know the banking system was busted, the economists figured out a plan to get the Level 3 bad paper off the banking systems' books. All they had to do was move enough assets to the US Government's books so that the system would be in balance, and no one would know or care. No one thought the US Government could be busted.

Over the past three or four years, the powers in control world-wide followed the plan. It was brilliant, and the banking system was saved, except for one small point. The sovereign governments of the world went "all in."

The powers in control graduated from trying to save major financial institutions as in the 1998 LTCM failure and an unseen banking crisis to saving NASDAQ companies in 2000-2001, to saving the stock market in 2001-2002, to saving the banking systems in 2009-2012. However, now that the sovereign nations of the world are all in, can anyone save the sovereign nations when either the money runs out or the bond market says "no more"? Can this ever happen? Ben Bernanke, former chairman of the US Federal Reserve said, "The US government has a technology, called a printing press, that allows it to produce as many dollars as it wishes at essentially no cost."[2]

I am not trying to second-guess the powers in control to say they were right or wrong. I do not know whether they were correct, nor do I judge them or their underlying motives. They have a difficult task, but I believe God's invisible hand in still in control and moving everything forward. He's working out things for our good, although in the short term, it may not seem good. The signs of the times seem clear: one day, the house of cards could come tumbling down, and this could happen suddenly like it did in 2008. The subprime problems were always there in 2005 through 2007, but they seemed to suddenly surface out of nowhere in 2008.

IF YOU LOST YOUR WEALTH, WOULD JESUS BE ENOUGH?

For the believer, we would love the answer to be, "Of course, Jesus is enough." Unfortunately, reality does not always intersect nicely with our faith. As with electricity, when a hot 120-volt line connects with another 120-volt line of a different phase, there is a mini explosion, and a giant fire can start.

Ponder the following questions.

- How would you as a husband and wife live if one or both of you lost your job(s)?
- How would you live if you lost your business?
- How would you make the mortgage payments on your home?
- How would you pay for your kids' schooling or supplies?
- How would you pay for your food, car, gas, or entertainment?
- Could you handle the changes in lifestyle?
- Could you handle just the threat of losing everything?
- How would you handle the daily pressure, not knowing whether the banks would approve the loan that you desperately need to continue life and business for six more months?

I know I would struggle and would not be able to answer these questions with a strong affirmative today.

THRIVE BY BEING PREPARED EARLY

Most believers might agree that we should always be ready for sudden disaster, but unless we go through hardships, suffering, and great pressure, we cannot be spiritually and emotionally ready. Paul says it well in 2 Corinthians 1:8-11, "We do not want you to be uninformed, brothers, about the hardships we suffered in the province of Asia. We were under great pressure, far beyond our ability to endure, so that we despaired even of life. Indeed, in our hearts we felt the sentence of death. But this happened that we might not rely on ourselves but on God, who raises the dead. He has delivered us from such a deadly peril, and he will deliver us. On him we have set our hope that he will continue to deliver us, as you help us by your prayers" (NIV).

Very few believers, including myself, would cherish going through difficult circumstances in order to grow spiritually. Yet, unless we go through these circumstances, it seems like we cannot grow our faith to become totally dependent on God.

The financial arena is one area in the Bible where God specifically tells us to live a certain way, and we can be prepared without having to go through tough times, like bankruptcy, severe indebtedness, liquidation of assets to pay bills, etc. We can follow a few godly guidelines and rest secure. Of course, the circumstances I describe do not take into account the blessings of God in your life due to His favor, His wisdom, or His giving through you because He chose you, deservedly or not. This is grace.

So grace aside, here are some of the simple biblical guidelines that may help us steer clear of any sudden financial disaster ahead. I add one of Hyman Minsky's practical secular economic theories to the biblical foundation of the fourth guideline.

Give God what is His, and be generous with your offerings to Him. You cannot out-give God. Do not try to give to God in order to get Him to bless you. God knows your heart. Why try to fool Him?

Don't spend more than you can earn.

Save for a rainy day, even if you have to force yourself to cut back on consumption spending in order to pay off debt and start a savings program. I will elaborate more on this principle, which I call the Joseph Plan.

Don't borrow, except to become self-sustaining. Therefore, a loan for a mortgage on a home, which will be your primary residence and is not overly ambitious in payments, is okay. Your mortgage can be 25-35% of your total income. A loan to start a business, which can be repaid out of the cash flow of the business, is okay, but make certain that you have a good business plan that is not called "blind faith." A loan to start a business or to make an investment that will only repay the interest on the loan plus a few pennies is speculative. A loan that requires you to sell assets to repay the loan is the road to bankruptcy.

John Mauldin's newsletter *Thoughts from the Frontline* said, "Hyman Minsky, one of the great economists of the last century, saw debt in three forms: hedge, speculative, and Ponzi. Roughly speaking, to Minsky, hedge financing occurred when the profits from purchased assets were used to pay back the loan, speculative finance occurred when profits from the asset simply maintained the debt service and the loan had to be rolled over, and Ponzi finance required the selling of the asset at an ever higher price in order to make a profit."[3]

I'll come back to Minsky's explanation of debt in Chapter 6. For now, it should be obvious that much of the current financial debt was based on speculative and Ponzi finance: the investment loans were never meant to be repaid from initial investment profits. Minsky believes all such finance is speculative.

ECONOMIC UNDERSTANDING BRINGS AWARENESS

There are many schools of economic thought today, including a few good ones and many bad ones. Application of economic theories can best be stated with the saying, "The proof is in the pudding." Does it work for sixty to eighty years?

The dominant economic theory followed and applied today is from John Maynard Keynes. He believed the powers in control could adjust the system and keep things in balance to create the least amount of pain. It worked for a while until it didn't work, as we now know today.

Proper application of Minsky's work, as well as the Austrian School of Economics (Ludwig Von Mises, Carl Menger, and Murray Rothbard) might have kept the world out of the mess that we are in today. No one can truly know, and it does not matter. I am not here to argue one way or another. Any good theory in the hands of greedy powers does not work anyway.

The Keynesian model, along with greedy powers in control, have brought the world to the brink of economic disaster, and that disaster may be right in front of us.

While you cannot control what the powers will do, you can control your own financial destiny somewhat so that their errors, greed, and oversight do not become your financial demise. Realize that any economic disaster will affect you negatively because you may still lose your employment, your business, and eventually have to make many difficult prayerful decisions. The more time you have, the better. The more prepared you are, the better. If your family is mentally, emotionally, and spiritually prepared, you have a better chance of surviving and thriving.

The Bible tells us some truths about banking in Proverbs 22:7, "The rich rule over the poor, and the borrower is servant to the lender" (NIV).

During much of history, anyone who couldn't repay his loan became a slave to the lender (the bank or the king). Today, people live under different conditions. People can declare bankruptcy, or seek help from the government. Without these fallback provisions, people would use much more wisdom when taking out loans.

As we move forward into the next ten years, we must recognize that these years have much more external risk than the period from 1950 to 2000. These were the golden years where income growth, investment asset growth in stocks and bonds, and housing asset growth were relatively stable and increasing. Periods of speculative or Ponzi financing were quickly corrected as the companies who made these kinds of loans eventually "hit the wall". Real growth in earnings occurred from one generation to the next. This generation was also able to pass on the wealth they accumulated to the next generation, making for an increasingly prosperous middle class. This middle class was the foundation of economic growth as they provided purchasing power, retail sales, and housing purchases, along with all of the products that accompanied new or rental homes. They also provided a huge pool of investment funds for business growth as they learned to save. They were the ones who went through both the Great Depression and World War II. They were what television journalist Tom Brokaw called the Greatest Generation. They were the working class, as well as the group that built small businesses all over America. Their hard work ethic, strong cultural values, strong family values, and the heritage that was theirs as American citizens were what made America's financial and economic system strong.

The current generation of young adults will be the first generation that as a whole will not be economically and financially better off than their parents. Something has drastically altered the landscape on the horizon that impacts this group of adults. Most Christians will recognize that the elimination of God from all aspects of secular life is to blame. I am not here to analyze the reason, but if we can recognize that there is a major economic difference between the period from 1950 to 2000 versus 2000 to the present and that this economic climate creates greater risk for working families, then we can adjust our lives accordingly.

A number of things can affect our way of life, namely our working income, investments, expenses, and bank loans. The Bible teaches that God gives wealth and the ability to produce wealth to whomever He pleases. That wealth looks different for each person. The income stream that with which God blesses each family with should be obvious over time. Projecting what that looks like is critical because it will help you determine spending and expenditures. The key to thriving is not financial wealth, but controlling spending and expenses, making solid investments, and wisely utilizing bank loans.

The mistake most families make is failing to have a budget. Perhaps, we make the mistake because we never learned the importance of budgeting in school or from our parents. We asked them for money, and they provided. Even if we worked as children, we had very simple budgets so that we did not spend more than we earned.

The Greatest Generation was very good at saving, which meant they controlled expenses. They knew what it was like to not have enough. Not having a budget is like taking a road trip to an unfamiliar area without a map. You will get lost. In the financial arena, you will likely end up living day-to-day, and if a disaster hits, you will not have enough savings.

In the area of investments, I know there were many people, including believers, who were caught up in the 2006-2008 housing boom and were sure they were going to make a "killing" investing in a second and third housing unit. Some lost a lot of money in the past few years, while some are still holding on to their property, hoping to break even. The famous dying words for investors are, "If I can only break even, I'll sell and get out." Some never get out. If the market comes back, and they are even, they think they will just wait for 10% more. From 1950 to 2000, you could do that and be fine. The next ten years may not be the same. No one knows, but the risks seem high.

You must make the decision. All I want to do is bring forth the view from 40,000 feet up. Take a global view of the current times, and make your plan. God has already blessed you with wealth; don't presume that He will bail you out if you get into trouble. He has already given us principles by which to live. Don't be a slave to your lender. As long as your job is secure and you have a plan for repayment to your lender, you cannot be a slave. Remember Minsky's loan classifications: hedge, speculative, and Ponzi, and finance wisely.

2

SEEING THE BIBLICAL BACKDROP FOR AN ECONOMIC DISASTER: THRIVING THROUGH BIBLICAL REVELATION

SERIOUSLY, HOW BAD CAN IT GET?

Alarmists, like me, have been crying wolf for hundreds of years, so what is the big deal about being ready? If an economic disaster strikes, God will protect believers, will He not? Maybe He will, but He may not protect us in the way that we think He will. God's greatest blessings are spiritual, but an economic disaster hits our pocketbooks and impacts us materially. The pressures to pay bills, buy food, run our businesses, pay for schooling, dance lessons, etc., are enormous and can bring severe stress to our families and our souls. Many believers will stand strong and adapt, but because these financial pressures will remain day after day, it will be extremely difficult.

We must understand the signs of the times by understanding what is currently going on and comparing the signs to a road map. The Bible is our road map. God has told us what will happen. As we observe what is happening today and note that things are lining up with what God prophesied, we can be better prepared by getting ready early. We cannot predict when things will happen or the exact way in which they will happen, but we can be prepared for the eventuality.

Let us see if there is biblical evidence for an economic disaster of titanic proportions that will affect the whole world today. If there is even a remote possibility, then this book's theme of being ready might make sense.

First, let us look at an important point. Does God foresee the future, or does God control the future? The answer is both.

CAN GOD FORESEE AND CONTROL EVENTS IN THE FUTURE?

To demonstrate God's foresight and control of the future, I will use an event that most recognize, the birth of Christ. Consider the following two passages.

> But you, Bethlehem Ephrathah, though you are small among the clans of Judah, out of you will come for me one who will be ruler over Israel, whose origins are from of old, from ancient times (Micah 5:2, NIV).

> After Jesus was born in Bethlehem in Judea, during the time of King Herod, Magi from the east came to Jerusalem and asked, "Where is the one who has been born king of the Jews? We saw his star in the east and have come to worship him." When King Herod heard this he was disturbed, and all Jerusalem with him. When he had called together all the people's chief priests and teachers of the law, he asked them where the Christ was to be born. "In Bethlehem in Judea," they replied, "for this is what the prophet has written: 'But you, Bethlehem, in the land of Judah, are by no means least among the rulers of Judah; for out of you will come a ruler who will be the shepherd of my people Israel'" (Matthew 2:1-6, NIV).

During Christmas, we see plays about the birth of Jesus Christ. Micah 5:2 was written approximately 700 years before Christ, yet Micah writes that Christ was going to be born in Bethlehem. Matthew leaves no doubt that what Micah wrote was written about Jesus.

Consider this third passage.

In those days Caesar Augustus issued a decree that a census should be taken of the entire Roman world. (This was the first census that took place while Quirinius was governor of Syria.) And everyone went to his own town to register. So Joseph also went up from the town of Nazareth in Galilee to Judea, to Bethlehem the town of David, because he belonged to the house and line of David. He went there to register with Mary, who was pledged to be married to him and was expecting a child. While they were there, the time came for the baby to be born, and she gave birth to her firstborn, a son. She wrapped him in cloths and placed him in a manger, because there was no room for them in the inn (Luke 2:1-7, NIV).

Luke writes an even more interesting fact about Caesar Augustus. He was Caesar of the Roman Empire, and he thought he was sovereign and supreme. Yet, Augustus obviously was a puppet in the hands of God, just doing what God wanted and needed him to do. Augustus issued a decree that a census should be taken of the people of the whole empire. This required Joseph and Mary to go back to Joseph's hometown.

Joseph and Mary were living in Nazareth but had to go back to Bethlehem to register. In truth, God needed this to take place so that Jesus would be born in Bethlehem. If the census did not happen, God's Word would be in error, and we should all rip those pages out of the Bible. In fact, if Jesus was not born in Jerusalem, we should throw out the whole Bible because it would not be God's complete truth.

GOD explains his position in Isaiah 46.

"I (GOD) make known the end from the beginning, from ancient times, what is still to come. I say, 'My purpose will stand, and I will do all that I please.' From the east I summon a bird of prey; from a far-off land, a man to fulfill my purpose. What I have said, that will I bring about; what I have planned, that will I do" (Isaiah 46:10-11, NIV).

God tells us throughout His Word that His purpose and plan will be accomplished. He is not passive in accomplishing His plan. He does not sit back on His throne but is active in causing all things to work together for our ultimate good.

ARE WE IN THE LAST DAYS?

Some of the spiritual truths that Jesus spoke are crystal clear to believers. The impact of spiritual truths on emotional, motivational, and material truths is less clear. As we live through trials, the clarity of Jesus' spiritual truths on our humanity becomes more evident.

Any discussion of what Jesus said about economic matters will be conjecture and speculation. Since my wife says I think I know everything or at least have an opinion about everything, I feel free to express my thoughts in this area. It's the reason for this book. Don't get upset if my theology or economic concepts, and how I try to weave them together, do not line up with yours. If you feel strongly opposed, don't send me an email. Write your own book. I'll buy it.

I will not try to overwhelm you with Scripture but will present Scripture references if you are ambitious and want to study them further. I will not list many passages merely in an attempt to build a stronger case. Much of what Jesus said in the area of economic impact will remain cloudy until God reveals His hand in the situation. In addition, any timing drawn from Jesus' thoughts will be an even greater stretch. Yet, I will try to tie in what He said about an economic disaster today.

In Matthew 24:3 (NIV), Jesus answers a question from His disciples, "Tell us… when will this happen, and what will be the sign of your coming and of the end of the age?" Commentators and biblical scholars vary in their interpretations of this question and the meaning of the answer that Jesus gave. I have my own opinions which I will limit to the economic impact.

Jesus says, "you will hear of wars and rumors of wars… Nation will rise against nation… There will be famines and earthquakes in various places… For then there will be great distress, unequaled from the beginning of the world until now — and never to be equaled again" (Matthew 24:6-7, 24, NIV).

From these passages, I conclude that the signs of the times are clear. The season that includes all of these signs signals the end of the age. It doesn't matter if the past two thousand years have also included the same types of events. These events are all happening now. I do not need to prove an increasing frequency or intensity of these events. The fact that all of these events are taking place now is enough for me to be ready.

THE CASE MADE BY JESUS

I believe the Bible makes a strong case for the return of Jesus Christ in this season, which could be in the next twenty to fifty years or so. I believe our children may see His return. Again, biblical scholars vary in their opinions, but I have my own thoughts.

My theory is based on what Jesus said in Matthew 24 and what Daniel wrote in Daniel 2, 7 and 8. This is rather complicated so I'll quote the relevant scriptures and then attempt to tie them together, presenting a case for Jesus' return. We cannot know the day, but we can know the season. The reason I start with Jesus' potential return is, if He were returning soon, we would expect many economic calamities just prior to His return. These calamities will prepare peoples' hearts for the gospel. The economic calamities will be of such magnitude that they will create a whole new class of poor, who will be rich in faith. God will ultimately be causing all things to work out for their good.

> "Now learn this lesson from the fig tree: As soon as its twigs get tender and its leaves come out, you know that summer is near. Even so, when you see all these things, you know that it is near, right at the door. I tell you the truth, this generation will certainly not pass away until all these things have happened" (Matthew 24: 32-34, NIV).

I believe Jesus was referring to Israel when he used the fig tree as an object lesson (see also Joel 1, Hosea 9:10, Jeremiah 24). Jesus was telling us to watch Israel. As soon as Israel starts to grow again as a nation, His return and the end of the age is near. When all of the things Jesus described in Matthew 24 take place, His return is very soon, "right at the door." Of course God's measurement of time is different from ours. "With the Lord a day is like a thousand years" (2 Peter 3:8, NIV).

In A.D. 70, the Roman general Titus destroyed Israel as a nation. On May 14, 1947, Israel was reestablished as a nation again. Soon after, its "twigs" started growing and its "leaves" came out. Israel became a nation again after 1,900 years. No nation has ever done that. Of course God knew that this would happen. He wrote it in the Old Testament (Ezekiel 36) and made it happen.

THE CASE MADE IN BIBLICAL HISTORY- DANIEL

The book of Daniel helps us understand the end times. King Nebuchadnezzar had a dream, and Daniel interpreted the dream. You may want to read Daniel 2 for a better picture. In order to keep this simple, I will reference part of the chapter and give my interpretation, which really comes from what I have learned from many

biblical scholars over the years. My point in mentioning these scholars is not to piggyback on their credibility, but to give credit to all
those who have studied and written commentaries before me. So at
this point, I thank J. Vernon McGee, Chuck Swindoll, Jon Courson,
Donald Stamps, as well as the Calvary Chapel network. I have gained
much understanding over the years from them as well as my pastor
Klayton Ko.

Within the following passage, I have included my interpretations by capitalizing them in parentheses. I state what I believe the
passages mean but will refrain from developing further interpretations so that the discussion does not become too complex.

> "You looked, O king, and there before you stood a large
> statue — an enormous, dazzling statue, awesome in appear-
> ance. The head of the statue was made of pure gold, its
> chest and arms of silver, its belly and thighs of bronze, its
> legs of iron (4TH KINGDOM), its feet partly of iron and
> partly of baked clay (KINGDOM THAT CAME FROM
> THE 4TH KINGDOM). While you were watching, a rock
> (JESUS) was cut out, but not by human hands. It struck
> the statue on its feet of iron and clay and smashed them.
> Then the iron, the clay, the bronze, the silver and the gold
> were broken to pieces at the same time and became like
> chaff on a threshing floor in the summer. The wind swept
> them away without leaving a trace. But the rock that struck
> the statue became a huge mountain and filled the whole
> earth (JESUS REIGNS).
>
> "This was the dream, and now we will interpret it to the
> king. You, O king (NEBUCHADNEZZAR), are the king
> of kings. The God of heaven has given you dominion and
> power and might and glory; in your hands he has placed

mankind and the beasts of the field and the birds of the air. Wherever they live, he has made you ruler over them all. You are that head of gold.

"After you, another kingdom will rise (MEDO PERSIANS – DANIEL 8:20), inferior to yours. Next, a third kingdom (GREEKS/ALEXANDER THE GREAT – DANIEL 8:21), one of bronze, will rule over the whole earth. Finally, there will be a fourth kingdom (ROMAN EMPIRE), strong as iron — for iron breaks and smashes everything — and as iron breaks things to pieces, so it will crush and break all the others. Just as you saw that the feet and toes were partly of baked clay and partly of iron, so this will be a divided kingdom; yet it will have some of the strength of iron in it, even as you saw iron mixed with clay. As the toes were partly iron and partly clay, so this kingdom will be partly strong and partly brittle. And just as you saw the iron mixed with baked clay, so the people will be a mixture and will not remain united, any more than iron mixes with clay.

"**In the time of those kings** (THE FEET AND TOES THAT WERE PARTLY IRON AND PARTLY CLAY) the God of heaven will set up a kingdom that will never be destroyed, nor will it be left to another people. It will crush all those kingdoms and bring them to an end, but it will itself endure forever. This is the meaning of the vision of the rock cut out of a mountain, but not by human hands — a rock that broke the iron, the bronze, the clay, the silver and the gold to pieces" (ALL THE KINGDOMS DESTROYED) (Daniel 2:31-45).

Verse 44 is critical to the understanding of the timing in the passage above. To which kings is Daniel referring when he says, "In the time of those kings?" We can easily understand to which kings

Daniel is not referring. He cannot be referring to the old Roman Empire, the fourth kingdom with the legs of iron mentioned in verse 33, based on his conclusion in verses 44 and 45. Daniel is talking about God setting up His kingdom and the return of Jesus Christ. At that time, God will crush all of the kingdoms in Nebuchadnezzar's vision: Babylon, Media-Persia, Greece, and the old Roman Empire. This includes all the kingdoms that now survive these kingdoms.

Daniel 7:23-24 tells us that there is a kingdom that will come out of the fourth beast. The fourth kingdom was the old Roman Empire. "The fourth beast is a fourth kingdom that will appear on earth. It will be different from all the other kingdoms and will devour the whole earth, trampling it down and crushing it. The ten horns are ten kings who will come from this kingdom."

I believe this kingdom is the current European Common Market. It occupies much of the same land mass from the original Roman Empire. It fits the following description in Daniel 2:42-43. "As the toes were partly iron and partly clay, so this kingdom will be partly strong and partly brittle. And just as you saw the iron mixed with baked clay, so the people will be a mixture and will not remain united, any more than iron mixes with clay."

You may think that too much time has passed between the old Roman Empire and the current European Common Market. Let's look closely at the following verses. Daniel 2:33 describes the fourth kingdom as having "its legs of iron" and the kingdom that came from the fourth kingdom as having "its feet partly of iron and partly of baked clay." Daniel 2:40-41 gives the following description: "fourth kingdom, strong as iron… feet and toes were partly of baked clay and partly of iron, so this will be a divided kingdom…"

These verses tie together and make a case for the feet of iron and clay to be a separate kingdom from the fourth kingdom, the "legs of iron." Naturally the feet and toes come from the legs of iron

(Daniel 7:23-24). Therefore, I believe Daniel is showing us that the people of the European Common Market are the descendants of the people of the Roman Empire.

GOD STOPS THE CLOCK

Scripture gives another example of prophecy fulfilled. Approximately seven hundred years passed between when the following prophecy was written and when it was fulfilled.

> The Spirit of the Sovereign Lord is on me,
>> because the Lord has anointed me
>> to preach good news to the poor.
> He has sent me to bind up the brokenhearted,
>> to proclaim freedom for the captives
>> and release from darkness for the prisoners,
> to proclaim the year of the Lord's favor
>> and the day of vengeance of our God...
>> (Isaiah 61:1-2, NIV).

Jesus quoted this Scripture in Luke 4:16-21 (NIV).

He went to Nazareth, where he had been brought up, and on the Sabbath day he went into the synagogue, as was his custom. And he stood up to read. The scroll of the prophet Isaiah was handed to him. Unrolling it, he found the place where it is written:

> "The Spirit of the Lord is on me,
>> because he has anointed me
>> to preach good news to the poor.
> He has sent me to proclaim freedom for the prisoners
>> and recovery of sight for the blind,
> to release the oppressed,
>> to proclaim the year of the Lord's favor."

Then he rolled up the scroll, gave it back to the attendant and sat down. The eyes of everyone in the synagogue were fastened on him, and he began by saying to them, "Today this scripture is fulfilled in your hearing."

Jesus quotes Isaiah, and applies Isaiah's passage to Himself, except Jesus left out the following phrase from Isaiah 61:2, "and the day of vengeance of our God…" Why? I believe it is because while Jesus fulfilled almost all of Isaiah's prophecy, "the day of vengeance of our God" was still thousands of years in the future. So we have at least 2,700 years between Isaiah's prophecy, between the "year of the Lord's favor," and "the day of vengeance of our God."

Isaiah wrote what God wanted him to write, but only God could see the differences in the times of fulfillment written in the passage He gave to Isaiah.

ISRAEL AS A REFERENCE POINT FOR CHRIST'S RETURN

I believe that Jesus gave us reference points for His return and the end times. The first is the rebirth of Israel. After all, the Bible is a book that details Israel's origin, development and future. The Bible begins with creation, the sin and fall, and then in Genesis 12, God reveals His plan to restore mankind back to Himself using the nation of Israel, to bring Jesus as the Messiah. The Bible ends with God still using Israel in the book of Revelation.

When God destroyed the nation of Israel in A.D. 70, the biblical clock written into Daniel 2:33, 40-41 stopped. It did not start again until May 14, 1948, when Israel was restored as a nation. The clock started again, and Israel was on its way to become fruitful as a nation again, where "its twigs get tender and its leaves come out." Today, Israel is a powerful nation.

THE EUROPEAN UNION AS A SECOND REFERENCE POINT FOR CHRIST'S RETURN

The current European Union had its beginnings in the early 1950s with its first formal structure in 1957 with the Treaty of Rome. The six founding countries were Italy, France, Germany, Belgium, Luxembourg, and the Netherlands. Notice that the European Union was formed after the clock started ticking again for Israel. I believe that the European Union is a second reference point in fulfillment of Daniel's prophecy.

The European Union countries are the "ten toes" (Daniel 2:41-42) and the ten horns (Daniel 7:24) that came out of the legs of iron (Daniel 2:33), also known as the fourth kingdom (Daniel 2:42, 7:23).

As we see today, the European Union fits the description in Daniel's prophecy (Daniel 2:41-43) in the following areas.

1. The kingdom will be divided.
2. The kingdom will have some of the strength of iron.
3. The kingdom will be partly strong and partly brittle.
4. The people will be a mixture.
5. The people will not remain united.

This is precisely what is happening in the European Union today. The European Union created its own currency in order to compete worldwide and facilitate trade amongst its member nations. The name of its currency, the euro, was officially adopted on December 16, 1995, and was introduced to the world financial markets as an accounting currency on January 1, 1999.

The European Union became a global powerhouse in its first ten years after the formation of its common currency. It has since run into trouble, and the result is a divided kingdom, which has some strength and much infighting. The number of people groups is more than the current twenty-eight countries that collectively call them-

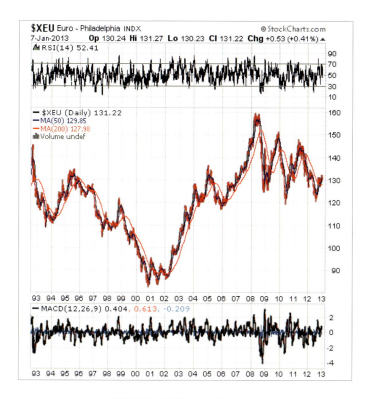

CHART OF EURODOLLAR

selves the European Union. Many other people groups have flocked
to these nations, and I believe they will not remain united for long.
Cultural tensions, financial pressures, economic pressures, and forced
austerity measures make for an explosive future.

CASE MADE IN THE BOOK OF REVELATION

The Book of Revelation begins, "The revelation of Jesus Christ,
which God gave him to show his servants what must soon take place"
(Revelation 1:1).

Let us examine a few passages that relate to impending economic disaster, not just the end times. Revelation is a very difficult book

to analyze, due to the figurative language used throughout most of the book. However, it can be a very simple book if you focus your attention on specific passages. I plan to focus on a potential economic disaster, which is very clear in Revelation. I will further simplify matters by not dealing with the timing in these verses. Since the focus of this book is to be ready, once you are ready, you will not be concerned with timing.

Most of us have homeowner's insurance for our homes, but we hope a disaster never hits. Whether or not a disaster strikes, you are ready. If you drive a car, you have auto insurance. You may never have an accident, or you may have one tomorrow. The point is that you are ready.

I will focus on Revelation 18, specifically the commercial and economical aspects. This chapter clearly shows that the world economy is in deep trouble.

Terrified at her torment, they will stand far off and cry:

"'Woe! Woe, O great city,
O Babylon, city of power!
In one hour your doom has come!'

"The merchants of the earth will weep and mourn over her because no one buys their cargoes any more—cargoes of gold, silver, precious stones and pearls; fine linen, purple, silk and scarlet cloth; every sort of citron wood, and articles of every kind made of ivory, costly wood, bronze, iron and marble; cargoes of cinnamon and spice, of incense, myrrh and frankincense, of wine and olive oil, of fine flour and wheat; cattle and sheep; horses and carriages; and bodies and souls of men.

"They will say, 'The fruit you longed for is gone from you. All your riches and splendor have vanished, never to be recovered.' The merchants who sold these things and gained their wealth from her will stand far off, terrified at her torment. They will weep and mourn and cry out:

"'Woe! Woe, O great city,
dressed in fine linen, purple and scarlet,
and glittering with gold, precious stones and pearls!
In one hour such great wealth has been brought to ruin!'

"Every sea captain, and all who travel by ship, the sailors, and all who earn their living from the sea, will stand far off. When they see the smoke of her burning, they will exclaim, 'Was there ever a city like this great city?' They will throw dust on their heads, and with weeping and mourning cry out:

"'Woe! Woe, O great city,
where all who had ships on the sea
became rich through her wealth!
In one hour she has been brought to ruin!'

"Rejoice over her, O heaven!
Rejoice, saints and apostles and prophets!
God has judged her
for the way she treated you.'"

Then a mighty angel picked up a boulder the size of a large millstone and threw it into the sea, and said:

"With such violence
the great city of Babylon will be thrown down,

never to be found again.

The music of harpists and musicians, flute players and trumpeters, will never be heard in you again.

No workman of any trade will ever be found in you again" (Revelation 18:10-22, NIV).

My point here is that regardless of your timetable, regardless of your end-times theology, it will be very difficult to do business during this time. Things are bad now, but they will suddenly get a lot worst. Trust in God is important, but just because we pray during an economic disaster for which we did not prepare, we cannot presume that God will deliver us. Our attitude in preparing for economic disaster should be similar to living a healthy lifestyle. We cannot eat junk food, drink coffee and soda all day, fail to exercise, and then pray and hope that Jesus will heal us if we have heart disease, cancer, diabetes, gout, etc. He could, but I do not think that He will.

Similarly, if we spend excessively, live with no savings, incur excessive debt, and enjoy Las Vegas and nights on the town, we cannot presume that prayer will cause Jesus to deliver us from debt and pay all of our bills. Jesus teaches us to be ready.

3

GOD PREPARED THE YAMADAS FOR THEIR MISSION SO THEY WOULD THRIVE

God will not send us on a mission without preparing us. He knows what He wants us to accomplish, and He knows what we will come up against. He knows the gifts and tools that we will need. He knows all. He has a specific plan and mission for all who sign up for His army. Each one is equipped in accordance with the plan He prepared. Some have greater gifts and resources; some have less. The one to whom He gives greater resources is not better or more loved by Him than the one with less. It is according to His grace.

When I look back at the past, I can clearly see God's hand on each one of my family members: my dad, my mom, Diana, and myself. This is not to say we are more special to God than you are. We are all special and He loves us unconditionally (*agape*), regardless of the task He gives us, or whether we obey and accomplish His plan for us. I can see that He prepared us for what He wanted us to do. He also had His hand upon you and your family.

For the Yamadas, that preparation was connected to A-1 A-Lectrician, Inc, the business that my father started over fifty years ago. Some may feel that I'm imagining God's hand is guiding the story when He is not. No, but I am connecting the dots, God's hand as I see it.

Proverbs 16:9 (NIV) says, "In his heart a man plans his course, but the Lord determines his steps." Each one of us had something in our hearts, some desire, some bias, some plan, which God gave us by putting us in a specific family. My dad's family and mom's family had a special blessing, a unique culture, a specific lifestyle and belief system that God used to cause my dad and mom to grow up a certain way.

This was no accident left to chance, and although they made their own independent choices of their own free will, God was guiding their steps, through early life, through their friends, through their difficulties, sufferings and pain. Yet, God was with them, even before He lived in them, working all their circumstances together for their good and for my good. God always had a special plan for me, as He does for you. I realize that I still needed to choose to respond to Him as He wooed me, as He drew me to Himself. We all have that choice to make.

As I look back in my life, I see His hand of discipline, and I see His hand of love, grace, and mercy. As I look back in the early lives of my dad, my mom, and Diana, I see a similar pattern. They all had times of joy, hardship, pain, suffering, and fear that resulted in God preparing them for their lives as well as life with me. If you are beginning to feel like I am the star of this story, I humbly say, "No, God is the star," but the story includes me a lot so I apologize in advance.

All circumstances resulted in an appreciation for family and a continued growth in character. When I look at the lives of these three people, my heart warms and my eyes well up with tears at the goodness of God in preparing them for the terrible times through which I put them. It is clear to me that God needed to prepare them, or I surely would have crashed and burned. Yet, each one of them reacted with *agape* love for me all my life, no matter how wretched, dumb, foolish, and sinful I was. I cannot even mention most of the wretched and foolish things that I did, but trust me, your lives do not have a leg up on mine.

GOD PREPARED MY DAD TO THRIVE

The Yamadas, 1935

My dad rarely talked about his life. Maybe it was because I rarely asked him about his past. I am sure that he would not have told me most of it anyway; his cultural upbringing would not allow him to do so. He was always setting a good example and would not have done anything to tear down my soul, which he might have done if he had told me about his past. I heard a little from my Uncle Oscar, my dad's younger brother, who worked as an electrician for A-1 A-Lectrician. I know he loved my dad Jimmy, as he would call him, because he

Dad at 50 years old

never said anything bad, but only spoke highly of him. However, he did tell me once that my dad was rugged and naughty when he was young. I also heard from one of the relatives that he was the black sheep of the family.

Dad grew up in downtown Honolulu on Nuuanu Street near Hotel Street. His father and mother came from Japan in the early 1900s and eventually bought and ran a mochi store called Yoshidaya. I remember visiting the store and can still picture the view from the ground level. The storefront was only about twenty-five to thirty feet wide, and they pounded the mochi right in the front of the store. The building had two stories with rooms upstairs, some of which were rented out.

WAR DAYS: 442ND INFANTRY REGIMENT AND 100TH INFANTRY BATTALION

World War II must have been a traumatic time for Japanese families. My grandfather (Jichan) and grandmother (Bachan) were first-gen-

Dad, 1941

eration immigrants from Japan as well as four of my father's siblings (Isami, Kazumi, Masaru, and Fumiyo). My dad, Oscar, and their only sister Yoshiko were born in Hawaii. The tension must have been extremely divisive during the war, especially the dinner table discussion when my dad decided to enlist in the war. I can only imagine the discussion.

Jichan, who only spoke Japanese, asked, "You are enlisting to fight against your mother country?"

"No, I'm enlisting to fight for my country," Dad replied.
Jichan wondered, "How can you fight against your brothers from Japan?"

Dad answered, "I have to fight for my brothers here. Japan bombed Pearl Harbor and killed many."

"What will happen if you kill one of my brother's sons in war?"

Dad responded, "I have to fight for my sons and daughter who will live in America. I have to fight so they will not experience the same prejudice that I experienced when I went to school. I have to

100B 442, with Uncle Allen

fight so Americans everywhere will know this is our country, and we uphold the family honor here. I have to fight for your right to sell mochi here in Hawaii."

"You could die in the war, what then? This is not our fight."

Dad stood his ground. "I am ready to die for my country, to protect America and my future family and the families of my brothers and sisters. If I die, I die."

Although this conversation never actually took place, I know all Japanese Nisei (American-born, second-generation) who joined the 442nd Infantry felt these ideals.

My dad joined the 100th Battalion, which eventually became part of the 442nd Infantry Regiment. He signed up in 1943 and was sent off to Camp Shelby in Mississippi for basic training. While there, the members of the 100th experienced much prejudice: they were derided as "Japs" because the Japanese had bombed Pearl Harbor and started the war on the United States. I know they fought with the "local haoles" (Caucasians) and even the mainland Japanese Nisei "Katonks."

The 442nd eventually joined the front in Italy, and my dad participated in the famous rescue of the Texas Battalion. While in Italy, my dad delivered mail, and one day he delivered mail to a Dickie Tanaka. He looked at the return address, and he asked Dickie, "How come you're getting mail from my home address?" God orchestrated a connection between my dad and a man who became one of his best friends. Dickie eventually became a source of information for me about my dad and the war. Remember, my dad never shared anything about the war, but God knew that I needed to know.

During the rescue of the Texas Battalion, my dad's job was to pull injured soldiers out of the forest. My dad was in a unit that handled cannons, but because of the forest, they could not use cannon fire. I imagine he went in multiple times, probably scared out of his wits, shaking in his pants, pulling the injured out to safety. I sometimes think, how did he do that? Was it courage? Was it pride? Was it the fear of losing his fellow soldiers?

I believe God was involved somehow. Because I love my dad, I can only think good and honorable things so this is my theory. In my imaginary conversation that he might have had with his dad, he said, "I am ready to die for my country… If I die, I die." This paradigm shift might have enabled him to press forward, past machine guns bursts, bullets zipping by, and the sound of men moaning as they were hit, pulling bodies out of the forest to safety. In war, attitude is more important than muscle, but the hand of God was also his strength, preparing him for the battle, preparing him for his future, preparing him for me, his son. Of course, none of these thoughts ran through his mind. He only could think of the task at hand. That was my dad. I don't know how long this battle lasted or how many he pulled out. I would not say my dad was a war hero as he was just doing his job. My dad always did his job. But I will say, my dad is my hero, not because of the war, but because he loved me and demonstrated that love.

The best demonstration of that love was his loving my mom. He also loved his family. The best demonstration of his love for us was that he worked sixteen hours a day, seven days a week, and when we misbehaved we would get spankings. Dad rarely yelled at me; he spoke softly and carried a big stick. When I became a dad, I tried to emulate my dad. I spoke softly (80% of the time) and carried a giant belt. He was also a master of creating memorable moments, and when I was about twelve years old, he chased me out of the house with a big wooden clothes hanger when my mom "told on me." That was love.

After the war, dad met mom and they had four kids: me, Ronnie, Brian, and Sharon. He started working as an electrician at AA Electric, and then eventually joined the Pearl Harbor Naval Shipyard. At this point, there was very little prejudice against the Japanese: they had won the respect of the nation. President Truman recognized the valor of the 442nd Battalion as the most decorated group for their size in the history of the Army.

Dad eventually started A-1 A-Lectrician in 1957 and that was the end of regular family picnics on Waikiki Beach. No more climbing on the cannon, no more weekends at the beach, and no more fishing or camping at Uncle Dickie's house. We eventually moved from the poor camps of downtown Honolulu to Pauoa Valley. Since we owned our own home, I remember working in the yard, building walls, digging dirt, moving the lawn mower, and raking leaves from the big mango and lychee trees in our backyard that shed a million leaves. The yard work was the best developmental upbringing that a young boy could have. It developed discipline and work ethic in me.

IS PAIN GOOD PREPARATION FOR LIFE?

I believe God took my dad to the war and was with him through the war. God needed to develop him for what lay ahead. God is doing that for all of us. My dad was not the only one special to God; we all are special to Him. I focus on my dad because this is how I see what God was doing.

Dad started his business as a one man shop. He would go up and down the streets of the Liliha and Palama areas of Honolulu, which was where the Japanese community lived. Eventually Uncle Oscar joined him and then Tommy, Harry, Fongie, and a multitude of men. Dad was a shrewd businessman and worked 24/7. He was the model of discipline and hard work. He slept for seven hours each night, and therefore, he worked seventeen hours a day. He always worked on something. He always had a new task for us. He was always thinking ahead. The most dreaded words I would hear on Thursday nights were, "You working Saturday." That was it: no playing for Jimmy boy.

There were very few words as I sat in the truck on Saturdays riding to work. His right forefinger always seemed to be moving in a circle, like he was taking notes in the air. I thought he was brilliant to be able to take invisible notes. How did he remember these notes? My dad was my hero. He knew how to motivate people, including his son. In elementary school, he taught me how to multiply 25×25. He said $5 \times 5 = 25$. Take the first number 2, and add 1, which equals 3. Multiply $3 \times 2 = 6$, hence 625. This unique mathematical pattern exists for 35×35, 45×45, etc.

I look back and realize these mathematical patterns exist because God created math and numbers, but at the time, I thought I was so smart in math. Thinking I was smart motivated me to study. More importantly, my dad thought I was smart, and I did not want to disappoint him. I never remember him putting me down for any reason. Even when I got into my first car accident (Diana was sitting in my '57

Chevy), dad didn't scold or rag on me. That was *agape* love. My dad taught me *agape*. God used my dad to teach me what *agape* was, even though we did not yet have a relationship with Jesus. God was always working for our good, and especially for my good. So it is with you.

MY EARLY A-1 DEVELOPMENT

I started working as a gopher for my dad when I was about twelve years old. We had a small business, and A-1 did whatever type of work it could. One of the things we did was to install small fire alarm systems in homes. They were heat detectors back then in the late 1950s, and looked like a two-inch-diameter white pancake with a button on the bottom. If a fire hit the button, the alarm would sound. I was the cleanup crew, as well as the one who loaded and unloaded materials.

Eventually I graduated to doing real electrical work and learned how to completely wire a house. I thought working during the summer was the worst of times, as it took time away from playing. Looking back, that was the best of times, as I learned about the business, about people, about hard work, about showing up on time, and just showing up.

During one of our company Christmas parties at our shop, dad received a telephone call. The steel plates that were covering one of our road jobs were shifting, and we needed to secure the plates. So dad sent my brother Ronnie and me to fix the plates. He gave me a five-pound sledgehammer, some steel pegs, a crow bar, and some traffic cones and sent us out. I can still picture the scene, which was on the main street of Kailua town. I was sixteen years old, and Ronnie would be fifteen the next week. It was challenging as we jumped into our flatbed truck, took our tools, got to the site, stopped traffic, and fixed it. The big deal was that dad trusted us on what, for me, was an adventure. When we returned, all he asked was, "Done?" There was never a thought in his mind that it would not be done. I was proud to be able to say, "Done."

Although I was certain that I would never work in the family business, I did join A-1 A-Lectrician in 1970, after graduating with a Bachelor of Science in Electrical Engineering from the University of Hawaii. I worked for a short time with Hughes Aircraft in El Segundo, California, but when I came back to the family business in Hawaii, I was "all in," totally committed. Dad allowed me the freedom to estimate jobs, develop our Engineering and Project Management Division of one: me.

After five years in the business, I learned everything and thought I knew everything that could be learned. I was ready for the big time, and since I was the greatest marketer and still had the best Engineering and Project Management team: me, I was ready to work with the big boys. I set my sights on Charles Pankow Builders, Ltd. since they were relatively new to Honolulu, and they seemed open to working with us. The other general contractors had long-established relationships with other electricians, and these relationships were difficult to penetrate. I thought I knew everything, but in actuality, I did not know what I was doing. Pankow took one look at our cheap price and quickly signed us up for the ride. They were not taking advantage of us, but rather, since I was confident, they worked with us. Keep in mind that I still love those guys because they gave us our start.

The years 1977 and 1978 were the acid test for us. I almost bankrupted the business, with two huge projects, Century Center and Makiki Park Place. Dad took twenty years to build the business, and I managed to almost lose it all in two years. Brilliance has its draw backs. The Apostle Paul wrote, "The man who thinks he knows something does not yet know as he ought to know" (1 Corinthians 8:2, NIV). I had always wanted A-1 to do bigger projects, and I thought we were ready. I was not part of his decision making process during that time, but dad went "all in" for A-1 A-Lectrician by selling his real estate properties and putting money into the business. So I sold my home and did the same.

Dad was always a healthy man, and he never got sick so what happened in 1978 shocked me. We heard from the doctor that dad had terminal cancer. The initial colon cancer had spread to his lungs. Mom was strong and believed that dad was going to get better. Dad kept bidding on work, and when he passed away in January 1979, he had secured enough work to last us for nearly the whole year.

The biggest lesson for me during this period was what dad did not do. It is hard to imagine what we both endured. For me, I went to work, day after day, and I knew that we were slowing bleeding to death. I realized this by the middle of 1977 when I started looking at our labor budgets. We had way too many men on the job, and I kept waiting for the crew to get through the learning cycle and get down the manpower curve. It never happened. We had all of our best men on the job. My manpower budgets showed that we should have had eight men at that stage of construction, but we had fifteen to twenty men on the job. When my budgets were at twelve men, we had twenty to twenty-five men. We were getting killed.

Each day I felt like a man sitting below the guillotine blade waiting for it to drop. In this case, the blade was my dad. I waited for him to call me into his office and give me the lashing that I knew I deserved. "Do you know what you did? You thought you were so smart! I have to sell everything I saved for twenty years!" But the blade never fell. Finding out that dad had cancer made it tougher. Each day I lived what Scarlett O'Hara said after Rhett Butler left her, "I can't think about that right now. If I do, I'll go crazy. I'll think about that tomorrow." I did not realize it then, but God was teaching me *agape*, unconditional love, through my dad.

How was it possible for a man, just fifty-three years old, with a wife his age and a daughter still in college, who worked for thirty years, twenty years of which he owned his own business, to hear the news that he has cancer and only six months to live? Dad should have had a revelation moment thinking, my son tried to make the business go, but obviously he doesn't know what he is doing. Dad should have thought that there was no way the business could survive without him. The thought, "I think I'll take all my assets, sell them, put them into the company and let my son be responsible for my wife and my favorite daughter," should never have crossed his mind.

I believe God was involved. I believe God prepared my dad all his life for the moment when he would transfer the business to his son. The period when I almost bankrupted the business was my Ph.D. program in running the business. When my dad's insurance agent asked dad about his decision to continue the business and why he never mentioned anything negative to "Jr.," which was my nickname in the construction business, never scolding, never saying anything, not even once, dad answered, "He knows!" He thought, "Jr. has now learned and will do better in the future." Dad's choice seemed like a foolish bet, especially when the situation should have dictated another path.

I believe that because dad went through a tough childhood, was a black sheep, saw death in the forest during the war, and struggled all his life as an electrician and a contractor, God prepared him for the financial difficulties in our business and the greatest test anyone can endure: can you love in extreme circumstances? Will you trust God in whatever outcome He decides? Do you truly believe God is sovereign?

I believe God's hand was guiding my dad through life, and although he was born again only a few months before he died, God was with him throughout his life. He lived through many difficult situations, and God helped him grow in perseverance, character, hope, and love for his family. Dad did not ever read the Bible or understand how to interpret it, but God was still working and preparing him for his ambitious son, Jr. The Holy Spirit was with my dad all his life, and in his final months, the Holy Spirit lived in him.

God had a plan for me to learn *agape* love from my dad, and although dad never used the term or heard the examples from the Bible, he lived *agape* for his family. My dad was part of God's plan for me.

DAD'S EARLY CONTRACTING LIFE

I remember two incidents from Dad's life that showed me how strong his character was. The first was possibly in the late 1960s. A contractor was renting the front portion of our main office on Mapunapuna Street. The renter disagreed with my dad over the use of the parking area. A fight ensued. The renter punched my dad, and dad went down. About five other people were standing around, but no one interfered. Dad got up, went into the office, and the disturbance was over. I remember Dad's cool calmness, especially after he was hit. He did not call the police or yell or swear; he just moved on.

The second noteworthy incident involved union head Blackie Fujikawa, a very notorious organizer and leader in the construction industry. There was a bitter dispute between Blackie, his underworld henchmen, and the electrical contractors. I remember hearing rumors that Blackie's thugs were going to electrical contractors and threatening them with force, bodily harm, and coercion. I heard about one incident where Blackie's right hand man went to one of the electrical contractor offices, and the contractor refused to give in. The henchman reputedly grabbed him by the throat, pushed him up against the wall, and lifted him up off the floor.

As we discussed the situation, I asked Dad whether he was afraid, and he answered, "Never ask the Union for favors!" He didn't reply concerning the fear factor. He just walked a straight line. Dad never wavered, and they never came around. As I look back, I believe God's hand took my dad through the war, face to face with death, so that my dad knew that he did not need to give in to petty concerns. As we say in Hawaii, "Don't sweat the small stuff, and remember, it's all small stuff."

GOD PREPARED MOM TO THRIVE

GOD MADE MOM TOUGH

Mom, 1940

Mom was born on Oahu, Hawaii in Pauoa Valley in the "Ice Mill Camp." Her father Toomatsu Taniguchi and his wife Hisa Ando Taniguchi were born in Japan. When my mother was born, Toomatsu, who was an educated man, thought it best for his brother Tsurumatsu Taniguchi to have a US citizen in his family. Tsurumatsu already had a son Michio, but he had been born in Japan. So my grandfather Toomatsu listed his brother Tsurumatsu and Tsurumatsu's wife Yoshi Matsuoka Taniguchi as mother and father for my mother, and they were her legal father and mother. In order to easily follow, I'll call them Uncle Tsurumatsu and Aunty Yoshi.

*Moms Family, 1923. L to R, Hisa, Nancy, Fred, Kazue, Florence,
Tsurumatsu, Takeshi, Yoshi, Helene, Toomatsu, Tsurumatsu son*

My grandfather Toomatsu grew up in Hiroshima and met his
wife there. Severe famine and war devastation in Hiroshima caused
my grandparents to move to Hawaii in the early 1900s. My grandfather was educated and could write in Japanese, so Japanese nationals
would ask him to write letters to their families back home. The Great
Depression began in 1929, but for the Taniguchi family, there was an
even greater depression in their lives: Toomatsu had appendicitis and
died in the hospital. That night was a blur, but my mother remembers
the whole family gathered around Toomatsu's bed, realizing that he
was not going to survive. Mom was only four years old when her dad
passed away.

After Toomatsu died, life changed for the Taniguchi family.
Hisa Taniguchi had four kids to feed with no provider. The oldest
was Fred, then Takeshi, Nancy and mom. Fred was a good student
and had been accepted to the University of Hawaii. However, once
their father passed away, that door closed. Fred couldn't find a job

Yoshi Matsuoka Taniguchi

after the stock market crashed on October 29, 1929, so he started hanging around with some unsavory kids. God used a police officer who noticed this gang of kids in the neighborhood and went to see Hisa. He told her what he noticed, and based on his experience, he warned her that Fred was headed for trouble and suggested that the family move away from the area.

The Taniguchi family moved to Kekaha, Kauai because Hisa had lived there when she and Toomatsu first arrived from Japan, and she still had friends who owned the Kekaha Store. Kekaha was a sugar plantation town that had plenty of work for strong backs and smart minds. Fred quickly moved up the ladder to eventually become a supervisor, and he was involved in the early movement to unionize for better pay and living standards.

As I look back, God's hand provided guidance, but the choice was with Hisa. God used a policeman who cared enough to warn her to move. Who does that today? This is part of how America has changed. Also, few families today would move from one island to another, going from Honolulu to a small plantation town. It was like moving backward, just to protect the family, but not to Hisa Taniguchi. Fred's and the family's welfare was the reason for living, and they all demonstrated love by uprooting the whole family for the sake of one. The move was a great sacrifice.

During the Depression the plantations paid low wages, but what some saw as plantation owners taking advantage of the workers, others saw as golden opportunities for a new life. As I look back, I can see God's hand was involved, working for Mom's good, making her strong, developing her character, giving her the qualities of appreciating hard work, never giving up, loyalty, integrity, honor, responsibility, and family as a priority. Mom always preached these qualities, but she also lived them as she raised us. She walked with us through thick and thin with a never-give-up attitude.

God was preparing her for me, for my development and my growth. She gave me *agape* love in spite of my "bad boy" life. She knew all my faults, all my weaknesses, what I was doing during my crazy days, yet she never criticized, found fault, or threw up her arms in disgust at my failings. In fact, mom never saw me as a "bad boy." God made her strong, and she was blind to my shortcomings.

Mom moved to Kekaha, Kauai when she was about six years old. Kekaha was, and still is, a plantation town. My brother Ronnie and I spent each summer with the Taniguchi family from the time I was four years old until I was nine. We experienced plantation life. The first time we went to Kauai, Ronnie was three years old, and I must have been responsible for watching him on the propeller airplane.

The summers were great times of camping, fishing, and swimming, and they were full of fun. Thinking about Aunty Helen, Mac, Uncle Take and their families brings back fond memories. I can still picture the house in which we lived. The town formed around a sugar mill and had one post office with no restaurants or movie theaters.

You went to the post office to pick up your mail because there was no delivery service. I remember that one of the Taniguchi cousins was excited because they were going to "town." I wondered what the excitement was about because I assumed town was Lihue, the main city on Kauai, but they meant Honolulu.

During that time in the early 1950s, the Taniguchi family did not have any toilets, tubs, or showers inside the house. If I had to relieve myself, I took a flashlight and walked about forty feet behind the house to a common outhouse toilet. My solution was that I did not drink any water after dinner. Two hours before it was time to take a bath, we built a fire to heat a Japanese *furo* hot tub. That was fun. I washed myself outside the *furo*, and after I rinsed myself clean, I got into the *furo* to relax. Everyone used the same water so I had to clean myself first.

Since mom moved to Kekaha twenty years earlier, I can imagine how they lived. The roads were all dirt, and since the area was extremely dry, dust must have been constantly blowing in the winds. Add to that the smoke from the sugar mill, and life must have been interesting. The closest school was in Waimea, and the kids often had to walk to school, a distance of about three miles. Walking makes kids tough. A lot of unexpected things can happen on the road, so you become tough, or you don't survive.

HIROSHIMA—GO BACK NOW OR NEVER

Around 1935, Uncle Tsurumatsu, and Aunty Yoshi decided to go back home to Hiroshima. My mom had a decision to make. She was close to Aunty Yoshi who convinced my mom to go back with them. All Mom remembers is that since this was her legally recognized family, she went with them. She doesn't recall much about this period, maybe because she made herself forget the experience or maybe because she is now eighty-eight years old. In spite of her age, Mom is pretty

Hiroshima bombed

healthy and still works at our A-1 A-Lectrician company three days a week. How is that for tough?

Mom remembers a significant event that happened while she was going to the Yamanaka School in Hiroshima. One day the teachers called the American children into meetings to tell them if they ever wanted to return to America, they needed to return immediately. Japan was going to war with the United States, and if they did not return immediately, they may never be able to return. They were informed during the spring of 1941. My mom took the long boat ride home and never looked back.

Mom does not recall much about her time in Japan or her return home, but I believe that God used this time to continue to make her strong. She was only twelve when she left Kekaha, Hawaii for Japan, and she was sixteen and a half when she returned in April 1941. She must have had a difficult time in Japan, not knowing anyone, being an American citizen, and speaking broken Japanese. She does not recall the other Japanese students mistreating her, but I imagine they might have. I attribute her lack of feeling mistreated to her toughness, like having a tortoise shell with which God protected and toughened her. If the Japanese girls did insult her, the insults bounced off that protective shell.

The boat ride back must have made her even stronger. She came back by herself and must have had tremendous turmoil within her soul. What would happen to her Uncle Tsurumatsu and Aunty Yoshi with whom she had lived for nearly five years? She was close to Aunty Yoshi whom she describes as kind and generous, always willing to "feed and help everybody." My mother was very close to Aunty Yoshi, and although Aunty Yoshi was like a mother to my mom, she could never bring herself to call her "Mother" or "Mama." She reserved those names for her mom back home.

She was the only young girl without parents on the ship back to America, but God sent an angel. A European man who had live animals and brought them back to America for the zoos became her friend, and she went to see the animals everyday. She remembers lions, tigers, and monkeys, among others. Mom called him Mr. Croakas. Since that was not his name, he would correct her and say, "My name isn't Mr. Croakas." They built a friendship, and the animals helped keep her mind off the events at hand.

When she returned to Kekaha to finish high school, the other kids must have treated her differently. In their minds did they think she was "Japanese" since they all knew she left because her legal parents were from Japan? Why did she live with her adoptive *hanai* family, and why did she come back? Did she abandon her Japanese family? What went through her mind regarding her uncle and aunt after the attack on Pearl Harbor?

After the United States dropped the atomic bomb on Hiroshima, what did my mom think? What happened to her legal family, especially the aunt with whom she was close? She does not remember.

I believe God made her tough, and she had to have tremendous discipline to put these thoughts out of her mind. This discipline and growth in character helped her thrive the rest of her life.

THE DEATH OF HER HUSBAND

My dad passed away on January 13, 1979. Mom has lived more years without dad than she did with him.

My sister Sharon tells us a story that she remembers of what happened when mom and dad went to meet the union pension retirement administrator. My dad was a contractor, but he could participate in the union pension fund since he was an owner/employee, as long as he made contributions.

Dad and Mom went to see the union pension administrator, and she advised them of their options. My dad chose an option that took his cancer and doctor's prognosis into account and would give maximum benefits to my mom if he were to die soon. Mom took control and said, no, that was not what they were going to do. They took an option that would stretch out benefits over a long period of time, but this would only provide maximum funding if Dad lived a long time. If he died early, Mom would get a much smaller amount. She took that option, knowing that the doctor had given dad less than four months to live.

This happened during the latter part of 1978. It was at this time that I had almost bankrupted the company, and Dad had already pulled nearly all of his funds together to recapitalize the company. Essentially, everything that he had been saving and putting aside for the family, for their retirement, and for Mom, had to go back into the company. Mom did not have additional money saved on which she could depend, yet she decided to take a pension option that was not a smart financial choice.

When Sharon asked Mom why she made that choice, knowing Dad's condition, Mom responded, "Dad needed to hear that someone had faith that he would be healed." Mom was not concerned with the smart financial move; she had only one thing in mind: her husband's faith. During this time they started attending First Assembly of God Church, thanks to Katherine Fujino who invited them. God had made my mom strong. All her life He was preparing her.

Six years later when A-1 got into trouble again, Mom, with no hesitation, sold the Nuuanu dream house that dad personally built in 1961 so that we could again recapitalize the business. She was not emotionally attached to the house, even though Dad participated in every aspect of its construction. God had made Mom strong. Did I learn anything over the years of business? Yes, Family!

MY STORY—HOW GOD PREPARED ME TO THRIVE

GROWING UP IN UPPER CHINATOWN

I was born in Honolulu at Kuakini Hospital. Dad was an electrician, and we lived in a small "camp" near the current location of Hosoi Mortuary. The streets were not paved, the houses were old plantation-style houses, and the roof was made of metal. When I was a toddler, the roof seemed to be alive. Sounds came from it: I could hear birds or rats as they walked on the roof, rain sounded like a machine gun, storms sounded like bazookas, and if it was windy, it seemed like the trees were attacking the house. At least, we were rich since we had a toilet inside the house that flushed when you pulled the chain, which was not very often because it wasted water. We moved to Pauoa Valley when I was about five years old, and the house was brand new with all the modern amenities.

Our back yard was large with two big trees, making a great playground. The front of our home had a steep driveway to the carport, and my dad, always the builder, added a larger carport in front, which doubled as our basketball target. We used the carport beam as our net; if you hit the right spot, you got two points. We didn't have a net

1ˢᵗ Home, View from Hosoi Mortuary

and didn't need one. We learned to make up and make do with what we had. The roadway was our court, and the few cars interrupted us as they passed through our court. The neighbors did not mind us playing on the road. We even knew them: the Uyetakes, Kondos, Sekiguchis, and the Weatherbees.

Two of my friends, who lived behind us, were Clarence and Ronald. They were my early playmates, and we did a lot of crazy things. They were both Portuguese, but I didn't know the difference. We played football, baseball, basketball, and our world expanded as we graduated to playing in Booth Park. I would walk to Pauoa Elementary School, and Pauoa Valley became my stomping grounds.

RISKS HELP BOYS DEVELOP THEIR SOUL

God placed me in fertile ground to develop and grow me. I believe that God made boys to explore and take risks, and that the more they explore, the more their brain and character develop for future use. Mom and Dad's values and upbringing play a vital role, but God's ways seem to require living in the playground to really be touched by Him. Learning cannot be limited to a classroom setting, where proper godly living is only taught. The biblical idea of training "a child in the way he should go" (Proverbs 22:6) requires wisdom and consistently demonstrating living and walking the way Jesus would and letting the child make his/her own choice. This concept is enhanced by what Dannah Gresh writes in her book *Six Ways to Keep the "Good" in Your Boy* (with my own comments bracketed).

> The prefrontal cortex of his brain isn't fully developed yet. This area of the brain takes control of setting priorities, forming strategies, controlling impulses, and pursuing ideas. It's a 'cognitive' thinking area, which also includes making moral decisions. This is your son's moral-value brake system. Sadly, it's still 'waiting on parts' until he's in his mid-twenties. Until then, he's got his aggression and risk putting part of his brain on overdrive. The engine is revved, the wheels are turning, but the brakes are likely to cut out when needed! He's going to have a hard time consistently making good self-control and judgment decisions…

> But there's a huge upside: The unique wiring of your son's brain poises him for goodness! [GOD'S PATTERNS?] He may one day take the risk to build a fortune 500 company… It may be second nature for him to kick down the door of a brothel to rescue a little girl from traffickers in India…

> From the age of eleven until his early twenties, a young man is learning to direct his aggression and

> risk-taking toward good. A fundamental component of this is what we'll call his 'call of duty.' [GOD'S PATTERNS?] It is the process of learning to direct his energies toward a fulfilling life mission.
>
> While a boy is developing his sense of a call of duty, it is vital that a dad try to connect with him emotionally...[1]

This may be another one of God's patterns in raising kids. God puts in a child's soul a "call of duty" from which He can guide the child as he is growing up. Eventually the Holy Spirit will tap into this call to mold him and bring him to his mission.

Kids will always have a measure of disobedience, but God convicts their conscience (Romans 2:14-15) so they know right from wrong and are drawn to right through that conviction. Parents will always have to trust God as they raise children since this process takes a long time. Parents would love for children to obey everything they tell them to do, to study hard, to grow up to love God, to not awaken love too early, to not drink, to not have sex before marriage, to not answer back or be disrespectful.

I know as a father, I used to explain to my son Jason what would happen if he started drinking, and I got upset at him when he did drink. Didn't he learn from me as he was growing up? Didn't he see what happened to his dad when he drove drunk and totaled his car? Wasn't he affected when I was drunk, told him to go to sleep, grabbed him by the shirt, and yelled at him? What does it take? Only God can work in us. Part of the way He works in children is to give them a sense of mission or cause. Dannah Gresh refers to it as a "call of duty." In spite of the wrong turns, God will work things out for our children's good over time. He needs our prayers to activate His actions in our children.

Maybe God has a plan that our kids want to have their way and their freedom without listening to us, and maybe that will force us as parents to call on him and not tear them apart each time they get out of hand. Maybe we need to learn from His Word that tells us how to handle a multitude of situations in raising kids.

DOING CRAZY THINGS IN PAUOA VALLEY

My mom and dad allowed me freedom to develop, although I don't think they knew about all of the crazy things that I did. They allowed me to develop and take risks, even stupid ones. However, knowing what I know about myself and boys in general, if I was trying to raise your child today, I would have a hard time letting him do what I did. Each parent has to find his own way, but knowledge from God is the foundation.

Although they allowed me to take risks, my parents were always there when I needed them from my birth until my dad's final days. In the early days, they provided for me in the seemingly small things. Mom always had tuna or egg spread in the refrigerator when we came home from school, even if we messed up. If she came home when my friends were playing basketball on the roadway, she welcomed them. Mom helped me with my homework when I needed help on the last night of an Easter break.

Dad was strict, but if I got hurt, he was the one to take me to the hospital, which was often. He took me to the hospital without criticism and without spanking me. My parents' support for me was unconditional, and I know that God used all of this to develop me.

God used my early experiences with Clarence and Ronald, and later another friend Mike, to grow me. I was about seven or nine years old when the four of us were playing in my backyard. One of us had a spear made from a broom handle that was sharpened on one end. Mike was a few years younger than the rest of us, and we were always picking on him. He was sort of bratty, so one day I grabbed Mike from behind, while Ronald had the spear and was faking throwing the spear at Mike, just to scare him. Since Mike was getting a little angry and starting to swear, I told Ronald, "Ah, go ahead, throw it, throw it!"

Here's a lesson: never tell an eight-year-old to throw a spear when you are behind the target. Ronald threw the spear right at Mike, who spun and ducked, and the spear hit my face. I ran home bleeding and can remember my dad's look of shock. He saw death in the war, but blood from his son must have touched a nerve.

We went to the hospital, and Mom said Dad almost fainted as the nurse cleaned the wound. I was screaming as four nurses held me down. I don't remember what else happened because I think they covered my face with a sheet with only the injured part exposed. Why is it that the crazy ones walk away like all is fine, while moms and dads endure the stress?

Another time, we were playing football, and Clarence tackled me. I went down hard and hit my head on a landscaping brick, splitting it open with quite a bit of bleeding. I now have a small crater on the top of my head towards the back. I think it was after this incident, which was in the sixth grade, that my mom and dad encouraged me to make new friends. Hence, my new group of friends was called the "Impalas," who subsequently became the "Safaris."

I didn't need much help to do dumb things. Once I was riding on a neighbor's swing, and I wanted to see how far forward I could fly. I did not know geometry at the age of six or seven so I was not calculating the angles. I went as high as I could and let go of the swing. Those of you who ever did that know that if you are almost at the top of the swing arc and nearly parallel to the ground, if you let go of the swing at that point, you fly high but not very far. I went straight up and came straight down on my back. God must have caught me, because after moaning for a few seconds, I jumped up, shook off the effects, and went back to playing. There is nothing like your friends laughing at you to kick your adrenaline into high gear.

I know God made the trees grow (Genesis 2:9). That is a pretty simple statement, but it is really a supernatural statement. Although it seems like a normal statement, God really grew the trees supernaturally. He said, "Trees, grow and continue to grow until I tell you to stop growing." Trees obey God. Little boys do not obey God. Of course, they grow into young men, who do not obey God either. I do not know why, but I loved climbing trees. I used to climb trees in the mini forest that God planted for me on Kaola Way. The forest is gone now thanks to development in the area.

I remember two trees that became my "friends." One was at the top of the small driveway leading to some houses just above our home. It was a normal tree about fifty feet high. I loved climbing that tree. As I grew a little older, I would climb a little higher. I climbed until I was afraid to climb any higher. Then I would sit in its branches, hanging on. The tree would sway in the wind, and I would just sit there. After a few minutes, the fear factor would diminish. I would feel a sense of accomplishment and climb back down. Time would pass, and the tree would call out to me, "Jimmy-Boy, climb me, climb me. Are you afraid?" I would take the challenge, and climb again, a little higher than the last time. That tree helped build my courage.

My second tree was a giant banyan tree with aerial roots that hung down like vines. Many a boy who grew up on Oahu and went to the zoo know what it was like to grab the banyan tree roots and swing from them. We did that as the highlight of a trip to the zoo. No one worried about lawsuits then, and Dad taught me how to swing safely. You just hang on and learn how to jump without falling. Many dads today do not let their kids swing.

Tree number two was my own personal banyan tree because it was on the right of the same driveway above our home. The problem was that the base of the tree stood five feet higher than the road. When I swung on the vines, my starting point was the high point of the driveway, and I swung out above Kaola Way roadway. This means that during the high arc of the swing, I was over the road, approximately eight to ten feet in the air. At the zoo, you are only a few feet off the ground, and you can let go and jump to the ground. On tree number two, there was no plan B. I had to complete the swing and get back to the driveway. If I didn't make it back, I was in trouble and in no man's land, swinging back and forth in space. Swinging was such a fun adrenaline rush.

One day, my trusty vine broke, and I came crashing down, falling flat on my back. God caught me. No one ever picked up the leaves that fell from the tree so there was a cushion of several inches where I landed. That was my last tree ride. As I analyze that moment, if the vine had broken a split second earlier, my momentum would have carried me out directly onto the road, and I could have been severely injured. Because the vine broke on the backward swing, I landed in a protected spot.

As I look back, these experiences were all part of my development, and they allowed God to mold me to become the risk-taker that I am. Sometimes that was good, and sometimes it was bad. My wife Diana loves me in spite of the risks I have taken. She likes the good and does not see the bad. God made her to be who He needed her to be so that she would love me the way I was until He could remold me to be who He wanted me to be.

God knew I needed trees to fully develop my skills, my instinct, and the prefrontal cortex of my brain. If my parents did not allow me to do stupid things and if God did not protect me, then my whole growth would have been stunted. I would not have developed the confidence to move to California after college to work at Hughes Aircraft for a season. That further developed my soul. I might not have been so confident and blind to the risk of contracting projects that were beyond the capabilities of A-1. Life might have been easier for Diana, Dad, and Mom because I would not have developed such a high tolerance for risk or been nurtured and disciplined by God after the resulting disasters that I caused.

I think I followed the same concept of living life with my kids. Diana and I taught them values but also allowed them to explore, take reasonable risks, and grow. We used to go to the streams, and I would allow them to climb on rocks at two years old, but I would be right behind them. At the zoo they would run and play, climbing everywhere, even with the risk of falling. We took them to judo, soccer, swimming, and surfing, even on relatively big wave days. They went deep-sea fishing and were out on days when our lives were at risk. "Dad, are we going to be alright?" "Yes, Jason, we'll be alright," I would answer, even when I really didn't know the answer.

I realize not many fathers can take their kids deep-sea fishing, but all can do something that gives their kids the ability to grow in risky environments. Do we trust God that He will work out things for their good?

CAN TELEVISION AND MOVIES BE GOOD FOR THE SOUL?

I did not watch a lot of television because life had too much to offer. Of the television that I did watch, I loved the comedies: Red Skelton, the Three Stooges, Laurel and Hardy, and Jack Benny were my favorites. I loved laughter, and these characters provided a funny, lighter side. Engineers need that. I also loved the movies and still do. Here are some of my favorites with quotes and lessons learned

- *Pride of the Yankees.* "People all say that I've had a bad break. But today I consider myself the luckiest man on the face of the earth."
- *Raisin in the Sun.* "Child, when do you think is the time to love somebody the most? When they done good and made things easy for everybody? Well then, you ain't through learning—because that ain't the time at all. It's when he's at

his lowest and can't believe in hisself 'cause the world done whipped him so!"

- *Les Miserables* helped shaped good values in me, and my all time favorite scene was when the French police caught Jean Valjean after stealing the silverware dishes from the priest. Tears always flowed as I watched the priest give the silver candlesticks to Valjean telling him that he forgot to take them and giving him his freedom. I wanted to be the priest.

Other movies shaped my wretched side.

- *Rebel Without a Cause.* I wanted to be cool like James Dean.
- *Gone With the Wind.* I wanted to be smooth and shrewd like Clark Gable.

I think that God had His hand on my thoughts as I watched these movies. The good ones established good desires in my heart. God also helped mold my heart even with wretched desires, like being cool or shrewd. With these, God allowed my sinful nature to motivate me to strive, study hard, work hard, and play hard. He used these traits later, to keep me going and fixed me when the time was right. This does not necessarily work for everyone. I had a strong family foundation with good values and hard work to keep me balanced. Without this foundation, movies and television can easily destroy the heart of young people today.

Movies, television series and advertisements today are much different than fifty years ago. The foundation of children's hearts come from the various inputs in their lives. Garbage in equals garbage out. Jesus said, "The eye is the lamp of the body. If your eyes are good, your whole body will be full of light. But if your eyes are bad, your whole body will be full of darkness" (Matthew 6:22-23, NIV).

Children growing up today have to keep their eyes closed to avoid being affected by the darkness in the world today. It is almost impossible to prevent bad light from entering kids' souls. Parents are not perfect, and media surrounds us. Social media creates a whole new evil entry point that can bring darkness into children, yet parents cannot effectively restrain the darkness by putting a hood over their kids through rules, laws, bribery, and forced morality. I admit I do not have the answer, and I can see clearly the challenge.

When I was growing up, movies and television had a lot of good content, which helped shape the light that entered by eyes. My parents did not have much difficulty controlling input, and their lives modeled good light. I owe them a lot for that and many other things.

GOD WILL HELP US RAISE OUR KIDS, IF WE LET HIM

Our kids are actually God's children whom He entrusted to us to raise. It would be a mistake to think that we own them, or that they owe their existence to Diana and I. Yes, it was Diana and I that God used to bring them into the world, but He created them, knit them together, gave them their spirit. When their bodies die, their spirit will return to Him. God knows the wickedness and evil that exists today, and He also knows what they will go through in life. He has given us many commands in raising them, but the first and foremost is to love them as He loves us. I need to remember that God is working things out for their good, and I need to help them to become like Jesus (Romans 8:28-29). In essence, God will help us raise our kids, if we let Him.

God trusts us to raise His children because He knows that He will also be involved. When I walk with our granddaughter Madison, nicknamed "Madi," around our pool area, training her to walk and teaching her about the dangers around the pool, I do not worry that she will drown. I grab her if she gets within one foot of the edge of the pool. "Danger," I'll say, and she doesn't get any closer. I think it is the same with God. He knows what is happening to His children every second of the day.

God also uses our kids to mold us, refine us, allow us to undergo pain and suffering as we watch them grow and make bad choices. God will guide them in their walk. Our tasks are to love them, to pray for them, to ask God to do what He needs to do, and to be the light for them as we train them. God also tells us that our use of the commandments is ineffective in producing righteousness in them (Romans 7:8, 24-25). Even after Jason had received Jesus, he found wine, women, and freedom (wheels) during his college days. Diana and I had many discussions on how to reel him in, but after I read and digested the book of Romans, I realized that only God could do that. I wrote about the way God worked in His life in my other book, *God's Hand in the Life of an Electrician*, so I will not detail the experience here.

The main point is that a parent's main weapons are love and prayer, living grace and faith in God. We realized that Jason was a child of God and that we needed to trust God that He would work things out for Jason's good. This realization was crucial to us waiting for God to work, and when He did, He enabled us to see how He was working and gave us the ability to communicate with Jason in a manner that enabled Jason to see God's hand working. There is no greater miracle than watching God work in our kids and using us to help give them His revelation. An even greater miracle is that God trusts us to raise His children.

GOD PREPARED DIANA TO THRIVE

The story of how God brought Diana and I together is already told in my first book *God's Hand in the Life on an Electrician*. If you bought this book and want to read that story, I will give you one free (while supplies last). Just pick one up at A-1 A-Lectrician, Inc., 2849 Kaihikapu Street, Honolulu, Hawaii. Just tell them you are there to get your free book. Your coupon is this book, so bring it with you.

Diana is the love of my life, albeit second, of course, to Jesus. God made her perfect for me in her physical appearance, her character, her perseverance, her stamina, her strength, and her talent for cooking. Her secret is in her anointed taste buds—she can taste her cooking and knows what to add or what is missing. She uses a base recipe, but as with any good cook, as she adjusts the volume that she makes, she knows how to fix something that has too much salt or shoyu (soy sauce).

He also gave her a servant's heart as well as *agape* love. Diana was born with a measure of *agape*, which God increased to prepare her for me. God knew she would be my wife, and He developed her for me. When my friends the "Safaris" and I had our card games, Diana was the cook, the server, and the clean-up crew. The girlfriends and wives helped, but Diana was the driving force. During the 1970s after we all got married, my Safaris friends, especially Keith, would always tell Diana she should open a restaurant or a lunch wagon. They also said, if I ever divorced Diana, they would all stand in line to marry her. This, of course, is Safaris talk.

Diana grew under tough circumstances. Everyone was poor, but the Enokawas were a little poorer than the average family. Both parents worked hard, but Pop Enokawa loved to drink and gamble. I did, too, and we enjoyed splendid nights together in bars listening to Okinawan music. In Diana's early formative years, the Enokawas did not have many material goods. Both parents were out most of the time, and the kids were left to take care of themselves. There were seven of them: Doris, Janice, Marvin, Diana, Hiro, Elaine, and Junki. Their first house was on Buckle Lane in Honolulu, where Kukui Gardens and Waena Apartments currently are near Aala Park. It was like an old camp house, probably built in the early 1900s.

When I met Diana at Roosevelt High School, the family was living on School Street, across from the Nuuanu YMCA. The family did not have much money, yet they were rich in something that I did not have. Their family laughed together all the time, and they still do at family gatherings. Maybe it was because they did not have much, or maybe because they had each other, they realized that was worth more than gold.

I remember the first few times that I entered Diana's family's house. I never thought it strange, but they did not have fashionable furniture. They had no furniture in the living room; you sat on the floor to watch TV. The kitchen had a wooden picnic table with a bench, like the kind you used to see at parks. They said they made it, but I always suspected they borrowed it one night from a park. I never asked them; when you love someone, there are some things you don't ask. It would not have mattered. The living room had a big long hole in one corner so they did not need a vacuum cleaner. They just swept all the dust, dirt, and small rubbish into the hole. In the back of the house, they had a large wooden crate into which they swept the big rubbish. When it was filled, they would empty the crate. The house was always clean. Cleaning is easier when you have less stuff in the way.

They never worried about roaches because the roaches were afraid of the rats. The rats never got out of control because of the animals in the house. They had stray cats and abandoned dogs around. Loving animals was part of God's preparation for the Enokawas, especially Diana.

Because there were three bedrooms in the house, Janice, Diana, and Elaine used to sleep together in the same bed, head to toe, toe to head. If you moved or turned, your feet would be on someone's face, but the Enokawas were a family so it did not matter. That was part of life. God was preparing Diana.

Doris, the oldest, had polio when she was three and one-half years old. That was 1939, and the world did not understand the disease. Ma Enokawa had her own story of how God made her tough, so when she needed to take care of her daughter, even though the

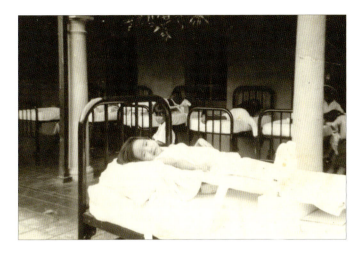

Doris in Shriners, 1939

doctors said her daughter might not live, Ma borrowed the money needed for hospital bills. There was no medical insurance for them. There was also no giving up, a trait that Diana has today. However, her husband at the time gambled away the borrowed money. Since he was already a bad provider, Ma divorced him and told the judge she did not want any child support from him. She raised the funds again, and Doris made it through her polio because of Ma's steadfastness and God's provision.

Ma eventually married Bert Enokawa, and they had six more kids. Ma owned a small restaurant, which is how she met Bert, who first arrived at the restaurant as a cook. Ma emphasized education and independence, especially for Doris so that she could become self-sustaining. This applied to all the Enokawas, and they are all outstanding members of society today. The family did most of their shopping at the Salvation Army thrift store, and it was through this connection that Ma sent the kids to their first church where they encountered God. All the kids went to the Salvation Army on Sundays.

Diana used to get Janice's old clothes, but since she had a heart of gold, she did not need fancy clothes to catch my eye when I first saw her. The sight of Diana wearing Janice's old faded brown dress woke me up in class the first day that I saw her; she had a glow about her. I think it was her light shining. I believe God quickened my heart and put a thought in my mind, "Diana is for you." I did not need convincing.

The family did not have food in their refrigerator or cupboard, but they never went hungry. Ma or Pop usually brought home something good from the restaurants where they worked. God provided. They also had their own early credit system worked out at the local market, located about one hundred feet from their home. If they were hungry, they went to the Exquisite Store, picked out what they wanted, and told Mrs. Yee, "Charge it." Pop always honored the charge. God provided. There were many impactful, real-life stories that made the Enokawas strong. They may seem funny today, but back then, they were life changing.

One day, Junki was trying to fix the main door of the house. In order to do so, he took off all the hinges from the door and then went to bed. When Pop came home, he turned the handle on the door and pushed forward. What happened shocked him: the whole door came tumbling down. Junki had not replaced the hinges, and now the door was damaged. For the next few days, they had no front door. In order to prevent thieves and burglars from breaking in, they all slept at the entry, keeping watch. It was just another day in the life of the Enokawas.

Numerous times as they were growing up, the utility company turned off the electricity, the gas, and the water. That was no problem and no reason to panic for the Enokawas because they knew how to turn on the main breakers and turn the gas back on, as well as the main water valve. The utility companies developed stronger quality control because of them.

Diana remembers a dream she had when she was about ten years old. Doris used to take her to Kress Store on Fort Street Mall. Doris used to make trinket bracelets and necklaces, and Diana would go with her hoping that Doris would buy her something. Diana's friends were also poor, and some of them would borrow things they needed from different stores. In Diana's dream, she was hiding in Kress after it closed, and no one was in the store. Diana was going to help herself to the neat goodies in the store. Suddenly, she remembers a bright light appearing and moving towards her. She turned her face away from the light but could not move. When she awoke, she knew the bright light was God coming to warn her. She never shoplifted, even though her friends did. God came to her in a dream and molded her character.

GOD SENDS ANGELS TO PREPARE DIANA

The Enokawa family stuck together and took care of each other. The doctors from Shriners Hospital told Ma that Doris would probably never walk since she was paralyzed from the neck down. God had other plans, but, of course, Ma and Doris had to live out those plans. Ma pushed Doris forward and supported her with nurturing love and encouragement. Doris eventually went to college and graduated from the University of Hawaii with a Bachelor of Science degree in psychology and attended another year of college to learn about medical records administration. She worked in that field for forty-five years. God sent an angel named Toshi, and they were married in the early 1960s. Toshi was a blessing because he was an uncle, a dad, a friend, all wrapped up in one package. He also had wings like an angel; he had wheels. I have never seen Toshi mad. The kids could "fly" to different parts of Oahu, and live life beyond their limited horizons.

Although Doris had polio, Ma made sure that she was strong in character. She encouraged her, pushed her, and cast a bright future

Toshi

for her in spite of her circumstances. Ma could do this because Ma Enokawa was strong. God helped prepare her and made Ma strong through the life she lived. God had a plan for the Enokawas and needed Ma to be strong for her family. Doris was nine years older than her next sibling so she helped raise the Enokawa kids because Ma and Pop were always working and came home late. Her immense struggle through her illness with polio and the resulting tough journey to get through school and the university made her the ideal "parent" for Diana and the rest of the Enokawa children. Toshi became part of the Enokawa family and was a critical part of their development and God's preparation for life.

Marvin is Diana's older brother, and I remember a story that Diana told me. Although it was not his fault, he had his license suspended and therefore wasn't supposed to drive. Diana was late for school and had an exam that day. She asked Marvin, and he refused at first. So Diana made him an offer he couldn't refuse; she offered

Doris and Toshi, Wedding Day

him $5 cash. Marvin was in the car in ten seconds. While driving, a lady ran a red light, and Marvin smashed into her car. They could hear the cries of a baby in the car, but no one was injured. The lady jumped out and told Marvin, "You're lucky I didn't injure my face; if I had, I would sue you." God protected them, but Marvin was now in big trouble. But the Enokawas always stuck together, and they still do. Without reading Scripture, they realized what Jesus taught in Mark 10:29-30 (NIV), "'I tell you the truth,' Jesus replied, 'no one who has left home or brothers or sisters or mother or father or children or fields for me and the gospel will fail to receive a hundred times as much in this present age (homes, brothers, sisters, mothers, children and fields — and with them, persecutions) and in the age to come, eternal life.'"

In Hawaiian culture, the real gold is the family, and any other resources needed are purely for the perpetuation and growth of the family. Everything in life is preparation for the birth, raising, growth, development, and nurturing of the family. The home, our work, planting, harvesting, investing, saving, and watering are things we build and do, but the real gold is the family.

WE WILL BE MILLIONAIRES BY 40; OOPS, WE HAVE TO SELL THE HOUSE

God knew the type of woman I would need. He had a plan for me and knew that I could not fulfill His plan without a strong wife. He brought us together, and He has kept us together. It is called grace. God placed Diana in the Enokawa family. She watched as Doris struggled through life, but Diana never thought Doris was struggling. She thought that is how you live life. You keep going. You never stop. You never give up. "Give up" was not in the Enokawa vocabulary. She saw Ma encourage Doris when it seemed impossible. She listened to the simple discussion on the importance of education. She saw Ma and Pop work hard and tough, never giving up even though life was tough. Even though Pop wasted precious funds, Ma never wavered and got discouraged. She kept working; she kept on pushing forward for the family's sake. Diana never thought life was tough. Working hard, striving, never resting and never kicking back were hallmarks of the life she learned.

Diana always worked, partly because the only money she would get was what she earned. The family did not have a slush fund or a college fund, and there was little money for elegant clothes. Diana's clothes came from Janice's closet. God provided by creating them the same size. One of Diana's gifts is serving so she excelled as a waitress. She could remember orders, she could add, and she was fast. She was working at Burgerland Drive Inn in Kapahulu on Monsarrat Avenue when a bus strike occurred in the early 1960s. She lived on School Street across from the Nuuanu YMCA. The Enokawas did not have a car, and Diana was not one to ask for help from Marvin. I think I was busy surfing so she walked to work. She walked from School Street, up to Roosevelt High School, east on Nehoa, down Punahou Street, east on Wilder, south on McCully, east on Ala Wai along the canal, north towards Campbell, then up Campbell Avenue to Monsarrat until she smelled the hamburgers. Diana was strong. She would not allow a small thing like a seven-mile walk to stop her from reporting to work. God prepared her for her life with me. She had to be strong and not let the small stuff get in the way.

After we were married, I told Diana we were going to be millionaires before we reached forty years of age. I think I told her many brash and prideful things. What man doesn't want to impress the woman he loves? But today, I pay the price. When we sit at the table, each reading our book or newspaper, and I think of something to share with her, I may think that I have a great God-idea or a great business idea, but she just thinks in her mind, "Yeah right, Dad!" She just keeps reading.

When I started work at A-1 in 1970, my dad suggested that I build a home, and I did so in Moanalua Valley. It was a cozy little house that we expanded because we had two Persian cats. The extension was actually a dumb idea, and the way we did it was even dumber. We added five hundred square feet onto the back of the house so one of the bedrooms became the path to the new family room. It really was unlivable, but since I knew everything, I did not need an architect. Dumb was my middle name. As long as it worked for the moment, I knew I could fix it later.

When we experienced financial dificulties at A-1 A-Lectrician, I had to go home one day and tell her, "I think we need to sell our house." We sold the house and put the net worth into A-1. Naturally, Diana had to pack everything for the move as well as move all of the boxes. Her key strength shined because she did not ask me, "What happened to your promise that we were going to be millionaires by forty?" She lived *agape*. She did not criticize or grumble. She just put her head down and plowed ahead. It was just another day in a life for which God had prepared her. This was not harder than anything she endured all of her life.

She could have very easily destroyed my confidence, motivation, and actually destroyed me. Instead her love and faith in me gave me hope and confidence for the tough season ahead. That is what great wives do. God had prepared her all her life for this move and new phase of life.

God did that with Ma Enokawa. Ma had her own tough life story, and as a result, she had the best work ethic of anyone Diana knew. She instilled values in Diana, not by talking, but by living. Ma trained Diana to be responsible. Diana remembers Ma saying, "We will never go on welfare or get food stamps. If people have kids, they are responsible for taking care of the kids." Ma did everything she needed to do to take care of her seven kids. She worked while there was daylight, and at night she worked by candlelight. She worked while she came home to feed the family, and she even worked while she slept! Diana disciplined herself and learned the value of work. God used Ma to prepare Diana for me!

THRIVE BY BEING WHO GOD WANTS YOU TO BE

GOD MOLDS US TO BE WHO HE WANTS US TO BE

IS BEING GREAT, REALLY GREAT? THRIVING THROUGH BEING SMALL

When I was young, I remember desiring to be great. I did not under-stand the difference between being great and accomplishing some-thing great. I would never have been able to understand, and more importantly live, with these two dimensions in proper focus if I had not understood God's view. My earliest recollection of wanting to be great happened when I visited the zoo and threw peanuts to the bear. I was approximately seven or eight years old and was throwing pea-nuts at the chest of the big brown bear that was sitting there, waiting for snacks. He would take any peanuts that landed on his chest and eat them. As mine landed on the mark, I saw two old ladies smiling, talking, and pointing at me. My imagination immediately shifted into high gear, and I imagined that one day I would be a major league pitcher because of my great arm.

I had a vivid imagination, but the problem was that as I imagined myself to be a great baseball player, boxer, or football player, my ego grew in spite of my non-existent talent. The first fight I remember getting into was in the fifth grade, and it was with a girl. She sat behind me and must have been hassling me, and I vividly remember getting up and punching her. She was bigger than me, but I hit a girl. Only a fool who thinks he is tough feels like he has to punch a girl. In sixth grade, I punched a boy named Melvin in the stomach. Melvin was the gentlest, coolest, most loving guy one could ever meet. Everyone liked Melvin. Only a fool who thinks he is tough would ever punch Melvin. Maybe I figured he would not punch back.

When I went to seventh grade at Kawananakoa Intermediate School, on the first day of school, I acted tough toward a small Filipino guy who was my size. I can picture him holding me against the wall ready to smash my face. I remained defiant even though I was scared. The only thing that saved me was his fear of getting into trouble on the first day of school. A few minutes after he walked away, I thought to myself, "Yeah, good thing for you, mister, or you would have been in trouble." One of my friends, who was already almost six feet tall and later became a police captain, came up to me with fear in his eyes. He told me, "Eh, you know who that was?" I said, "No, who?" He said, "That was Cecio, third bull of the school. You better cool it." Only a fool who thinks he is tough walks around acting like he is tough when he is only a skinny Japanese kid who is only four feet ten inches tall and weighs less than one hundred pounds.

I was in intermediate school when another small Japanese kid who was about my size made me angry about something, and we met after school to "beef" or fight. A crowd gathered, and I remember thinking, once I beat him, everyone would know how tough I was. I threw my books down, assumed the position, jumped around like I had seen boxers jump, and bounced my hands up and down, circling him like a lion, shaking my head back and forth. I don't even remember him swinging, but I remember being knocked to the ground with one punch. I got up thinking he had merely made a lucky punch and ready to throw punches at him. Just then, a teacher drove his car towards the crowd and everyone, myself included, started running. I was leading the pack. God sent an angel, the teacher who disrupted the fight. I wish I could say that I eventually settled into reality, but since I had an imagination that continually played the movie in my mind, I did not stop trying to be tough. The process of God healing me of myself took longer.

I realize God was working things for my good, and when I look back, I see that he used the YMCA club that I joined, the Impalas, which later became the Safaris, and sports. Sports help kids who are not individually talented to win if they play as a team. It also helps develop additional character traits, as long as parents reinforce them. I used to think that I was pretty good because I was better than my younger brother Ronnie at every sport we played. That was not a good way to measure my talent, but when you are a fool, you measure things to your advantage. When I joined the Impalas, reality and truth met my soul. I was not very good at football, baseball, or basketball, although we all played. As a team, we did quite well against the other YMCA teams, as well as Young Buddhist Association clubs. I started to realize there were people who played much better and were much more talented than I. They were bigger, faster, stronger, and more coordinated, and they played league sports and later played for local high schools.

Mike Kawamoto was the leader for the Safaris, and he would schedule games for us. One Saturday, we had a softball game at Ala Moana Park. We had one too many players, and Mike, who did the assignments, had no position for me to play, which meant that I would sit out. When you think you are good, you think you should play. I spoke up. Mike asked me whom I should replace. I told him Alvin Satogata. Mike said, "No way." Eventually Mike put me in right field.

The other team had all right-handed hitters, and Mike figured that no one would hit the ball to right field. Well, God had other plans to humble me so someone hit to me. Everyone was yelling out to me, "Hold it, hold it." Everyone on our team knew if I threw the ball, I would throw it "somewhere over the rainbow." Everyone knew except me. I figured I would get somebody out, somewhere, somehow. I threw it as hard as I could, and our team started moaning while the other team cheered. I cannot remember playing softball after that game. I think Mike stopped calling me, or maybe I was with Diana, and being with her was better than the humiliation of being the worst player for the Safaris.

In high school, I shifted my focus from being tough to being smart. I realized I had a certain gift, especially in math and science. Reading and communication were not my best subjects so I concentrated on my strengths. Unfortunately, my disease of wanting greatness shifted to my schoolwork, which was good and bad. The good part was that I studied hard. The bad part was that I still wanted to be great. I set my sights on being an engineer, and I decided I would attend the University of Hawaii to major in electrical engineering. I figured I could be great in this area.

God used my goal to make me focused. God is always working things out for us, and he uses what little we may offer. Although I studied diligently, I never really was a strong student, earning some A's and mostly B's. In spite of my abilities, the response from my mom and dad was extremely positive. They never criticized me for not doing better or compared me with Ronnie who had straight A's and a B now and then. When Ronnie and I compared notes on who was better, I always said that I had the better personality. In my mind, I always won because I made up the scoring system as I went along in the game of life, which could be dangerous for one's soul.

Getting good grades in school has very little to do with ultimate wisdom, street smarts, or character traits like respect, responsibility, integrity, and humility. Good grades may actually work against these important life traits. You may become proud of your intelligence and lack humility or respect for people because you think you are better than they are. You may lack integrity if you drive toward success at all costs. God help anyone that gets in your way. God help anyone that fails for the first time ten to twenty years down the road.

My help came from the Lord via his angels, my dad, mom, and Diana. Through all of my failures, car crashes, alcoholic binges, marajuana parties, and things I cannot mention, my family exhibited complete unconditional *agape* love. They let God be God and let Him be my teacher in changing me. No one could have accomplished this change in me, other than God. I am still far from the perfection for which I now strive. Diana knows and keeps me honest.

At A-1 A-Lectrician, God gave and God took away. God blessed our business, and God eventually took away when we almost lost everything. As I make these types of statements, God did not purposely cause the business to fail, but somehow He worked so that we got the contracts. He may have influenced me with the idea, or He may have opened doors to Charles Pankow and Associates, which helped me secure the projects. One way or another, I believe He somehow blessed and took away. He continued to do that in the mid 1980s when A-1 went through another tough period. As I look back, the message God clearly sent me was that He creates wealth and gives it to whom He pleases (Ecclesiastes 2:26, Deuteronomy 8:18). Much of the wealth that we create is made possible through the abilities He gives us and through the wisdom He provides as we depend on Him. God downloaded the plans for the magnificent temple into the mind and soul of David (1 Chronicles 28:12, 19). If I have any good ideas, brilliant strategies, earth-shaking methods, or dazzling organizational structures, they come from the Lord.

As I move forward, I realize what Isaiah said is true, "Lord, you establish peace for us; all that we have accomplished you have done for us" (Isaiah 26:12, NIV). This understanding is freeing since I am free from trying so hard to do great things and to be great. Once I realize only God is great, I can thrive in being seemingly small. I also realize He can do great things through the people He chooses.

GOD HELPED ME DEVELOP HUMILITY: THRIVING THROUGH HUMILITY

God used our customers to develop humility in me. In our electrical contracting business, anything that can go wrong usually does. Even when you plan, set up processes and methods, or develop flow and organizational charts, something always goes awry. I have had many calls from the General Contractors.

1. During the early phases of construction as we were trying to set up temporary power, an angry customer demanded, "Junior (my construction name), when are we getting power?"

2. During any one of many construction pourings of concrete, many contractors have called to say, "Junior, you need more men out here. We're about to bury you," meaning that they will pour concrete without all of our electrical conduits installed.

3. On jobs that rain, our electrician will go home, but then the rain stops. "Junior, where are your @#*% electricians?"

4. "Junior, what the @#*% you are saying about me? Are you accusing me of bid shopping? You know who I am? We did $40 million last year. Who the @#*% do you think you are?"

5. "Junior, where the @#*% is our fire alarm test? We are trying to get our Certificate of Occupancy and cannot get it until your @#*% fire alarm system test is complete."

Construction is an excellent environment in which to develop humility or to go insane. Customers can yell and swear at you, but they also provide your livelihood, and since they are usually right, in that your people, suppliers and subcontractors are the ones who made a mistake, you should not say anything, even if they are wrong. I have learned to zip my mouth, and as I have practiced not striking back with sharp piercing words, I have learned a little humility. After forty years in the business, normal emergencies seem do not seem as significant. Normal stressful situations do not upset me like they once did. Pain and suffering are good for the soul, as long as you keep your focus.

Why did verbal attacks by my customers or from someone who told me off, or cut me off on the freeway affect me so much previously? I want to have the last word. I want to humble others, not be humbled by biting my tongue. When they get the last word or action, put me down, or take what is mine and I cannot react, I suffer because my pride was destroyed. I dreamed of being a great pitcher or fighter. However, God's plan is to allow suffering for His sake, which develops humility when we voluntarily try to make ourselves nothing. This is good for us.

The Apostle Paul wrote that we should be happy when we suffer because that helps us develop perseverance, which helps us develop character, which helps us develop hope (in Christ, so we can rely on Him more and more), which then helps us develop *agape* love for God and *agape* love for others (Romans 5:3-5).

Also, as I look back I see God's Hand not just in my life but also in the lives of dad, mom, Diana, and my kids. He was always with us. He was always working for our good and for my good. I have learned I can trust Him more and more, although I am still a little child in my growth. I know there are a lot of challenges still to come in my life that I will have a difficult time handling, and they will be above my comfort level. They will involve things very dear to my heart. I do not know what they are yet, but I anxiously await the future because I know He will be with me.

Knowing that I do not need to fight back is freeing for my soul. I can thrive through my life's struggles without having to worry about how I look and knowing that He will walk with me on the journey. I hope to be able to walk humbly like Jesus did knowing that He is pleased if I can walk like Him. (Just a little).

GOD HEALED ME OF THINKING THAT I KNOW EVERYTHING: THRIVING THROUGH THE REVELATION THAT I DON'T KNOW EVERYTHING

Diana would tell you that Jimmy thinks he knows everything, or more precisely, "Jimmy knows a little bit about everything." There is a big difference between knowing everything and thinking that you know everything when in reality you know only a little. The problem with my brain is that if I know a little, I think I know a lot, especially if I know a little more than you do. I was certain that A-1 was ready for the big time and had the ability to do big projects.

I did not know or refused to believe that although we had good, dedicated, talented people, they did not yet have experience in the kind of construction methods that Charles Pankow used for their projects. It was like a high school football team thinking they were ready to play in the pros. Charles Pankow used slip forms, jump forms, and flying forms with which we were unfamiliar. They had accelerated schedules that resulted in pouring a new floor every three or four days. This determined the type of electrical planning and engineering, as well as our methods of running our conduits. They didn't allow us to penetrate their forms, which created havoc for us and was costly as far as labor. Our foremen did not know to what they should adapt or to what they should say, "No, we're not living with that." They did not have the relationships with the general contractors, superintendents, and foremen as well as the other subcontractors to make our work easier and less costly for us.

The real problem was not with my foremen, but the problem was with me thinking we could build with the big boys without really developing all these systems, relationships, and processes. It was my job to know, but I didn't know what we at A-1 didn't know. If you know you do not know, you start with smaller projects, you develop relationships slowly, and you allow your crew to learn over time. When you are anxious and think you know it all, you do not develop all of these things before you jump in.

One of the best things God did for me was to bring me into contact with my guru Peter Drucker. God knew I was not open to Jesus Christ and the gospel so he led me to Drucker. When I read his books on management, I became a management expert. I read several of his books, and I thought I knew everything about business. I had a dream to be the biggest, and the way to do that was to buy companies through company stock. I had read about high-flying corporate finance companies using their stock to buy other companies, and I thought we should do that. This idea led me to Drucker since I needed to understand management in order to build a conglomerate. I eventually started a computer software firm called Management Controls, Inc. Through this firm, we provided management skills, job costing, and project management, and we located firms that had the same philosophy and also wanted to expand their business. I was excited when two firms signed on with us, and we were off and running.

We started our software firm about the same time that we started our two big projects, Century Center and Makiki Park Place. I pictured myself as a highflying executive ready to take on the world. A year later, after both of the firms that signed on with Management Controls experienced financial difficulty and eventually closed, A-1 also got into trouble, and my balloon burst. Not only was I not able to use A-1 stock to buy anyone, the A-1 stock was actually worthless until my dad went "all-in". I soon realized that I really didn't know anything. I had a rude awakening, but it was the best thing to realize that the little that I know amounts to nothing in the real world. In Hawaiian pidgin, "Eating humble pie very healthy for the soul."

At this time instead of giving advice to everyone, I realized I should roll up my sleeves and get to work building our business. I jumped in and actually started to apply Drucker's principles to our business, starting with detailed engineering and planning, to the pre-fabrication process, to actually working with those in the field to set up better processes. I started supporting our field personnel in the things they needed to enable them to do their jobs better, rather than purely giving advice about performance metrics that were meaningless to them.

Previously, I had dumped job costs reports that were hundreds of sheets long into the job trays of my field personnel so that they would know where their budgets were. No one read the reports so I thought I needed to push everyone to read the reports. I preached to them the importance of the paper, when in reality the paper was meaningless. All that changed when we started to "live Drucker" rather than "preach Drucker." The same principle could apply to believers and their families today.

The crucial difference was that rather than me assuming I knew what they should do and how they should do it, I realized that I did not know. Therefore, I started to find out what they needed from me in order to do their jobs better. I worked with their needs and supported them in a new way. I also realized that my dream of being the biggest and the baddest went out the window. There is nothing better than a dream intersecting with reality for the soul of an ambitious dreamer.

I also realized that what I was really after was being thought of as the greatest. I realized I was a fool for trying to get there. Now that I am healed at least a little of thinking I know everything, I can thrive in a world where I know I do not know how A-1 will survive. Besides, my son Jason is now running the business, and it is his problem. I can thrive in spite of not knowing what will happen because I know the One Who does, and I know He will work things out for Jason's good. I pray he does not need a double dose of humility.

KNOWING EVERYTHING CAN BE HAZARDOUS IN AN ECONOMIC DISASTER: THRIVING THROUGH LEARNING

I am sixty-five years old as I write this. I thank God that my mind is still ticking, while my body seems to have run out of spare parts. I wake up with sprains in parts of my body that had no activity. I know Diana did not attack me. I know it was not anything I did the previous day. The other day, I woke up with a sore knee that I might have injured during exercise. I work out to stay strong, get injured in the process, but do not even know which exercise caused the injury. I had a foot injury that I noticed while walking our dog Piko. I have no idea how it happened. At least I know it happens, and my body is getting old and weak.

The feedback from the life plans that we follow is not as simple. The body knows immediately if it has pain. The soul takes a long time to adjust to the wrong choice originating from the mind. Working against the mind is our heart, which has pride at the center of its operating system. Most of my life, I was sure about things, proceeded with an arrogant certainty, and paid the price later.

Our heart's pride neutralizes any pain that results from a bad choice, wrong call, or incorrect assessment of circumstances or people. When I was actively investing in securities (stocks, futures, hedges, etc.), I studied, did research, and then plunged. I always resolved to hedge my positions, had loss protection plans, and made numerous backup plans. Yet, it always seemed that if a major position that I was certain would pay off or protect us went awry, I did not follow my backup plan, but moved to one of many alternative plans.

If I am losing you, let me simplify. When I was wrong, I always changed my plan so that I became right. I rationalized. I made excuses. I thought to myself that it would be okay in the long run. I never thought that in the long run I would be dead. If I made a bad decision, I stayed with that plan thinking that eventually something good would happen. When I line up biblical theology with my reality, I realize God was causing all things to work together for my good (Romans 8:28). However, it would be foolish to say that we can do foolish things because God will work it for our good.

We do not walk into a fight between two cats or two dogs. We know that would be foolish, but we do other things that are foolish. Not having homeowners insurance on our homes would be foolish. Not preparing for calamity is foolish. Not preparing our families for a possible economic disaster because we are sure we can maneuver through it is foolish. Our contingency plans may not protect us. Preparing now before disaster happens might be a wise idea. The type of preparation will vary based on each person's individual circumstances. However, there are some basic foundational concepts laid out for us in the Bible. We will look at some of them later. For now, we can set in stone the truth that we may not be prepared for an economic disaster if it were to happen next week, next month, or next year. We must decide in our minds that we will prepare. We might even thrive through such a disaster.

GOD KNOWS EVERYTHING SO ALIGN WITH HIM: THRIVE WITH HIM

I found that God never gave me precise straightforward directions. He worked on my heart, and then as I realigned my heart towards Him, He guided my steps. I guess if He made the journey clear for me, I would not have started. Knowing the journey all at once would have been too difficult, too large, too much work, and would have led away from my desired path. He placed some desirable crumbs along my journey, and as I nibbled on them, I walked in the direction of His food. As I moved closer to Him, God showed up, and I could see His Hand leading me as I walked.

My life at A-1 was the most important preparatory journey of my career. I spent the first twenty years doing it my way, and the second twenty years following God's guidance. As I look back on over forty years of life with A-1, it is obvious God's Hand was guiding me, and also the company, even before I came into a relationship with Jesus, but life was different once I found Jesus in 1993. As I look back on the past twenty years, I realize wisdom comes from God, and it is by His grace that we gain His insight.

The Bible tells us that God gives wisdom, but one passage in particular gives me clarity. "Then David gave his son Solomon the plans for the portico of the temple, its buildings, its storerooms, its upper parts, its inner rooms and the place of atonement. **He gave him the plans of all that the Spirit had put in his mind** for the courts of the temple of the Lord and all the surrounding rooms, for the treasuries of the temple of God and for the treasuries for the dedicated things. **'All this,' David said, 'I have in writing from the hand of the Lord upon me, and he gave me understanding in all the details of the plan'"** (1 Chronicles 28:11-12, 19, NIV, emphasis my own).

God gave King David the detailed architectural plans for the temple so that David would construct the temple exactly the way God wanted. This means that as we depend on the Lord, He can help us in our businesses, whether we are workers, managers, vice presidents, or owners. The way He does this will be different from the way He helped David. I believe there is a common criterion for this help. We need to ask, trust, depend, and look to Him for help. God will not help those that do not seek help. It also helps to be on the mission He gave us. For some, it might be to raise the next Billy Graham, who God will use to do something great. Keep in mind, it wasn't Billy Graham's great gifts and talents, but it was God using Billy as His spokesperson.

For others it may be something that no one will ever notice, but they are faithful to God as that is the mission He gave them. God honors them as they do their part in the body (1 Corinthians 12:24). For others, it may be doing an excellent job as they work and serve God as a construction worker, as a cook, or as a single mother desperately trying to keep God at the center of her dysfunctional family.

The key point for us to remember is that God is more interested in who we are than what we do or how successful we are. He is concerned about our growth and relationship with Him rather than us becoming prosperous from the wisdom He gives. He is not interested in enriching us unless He has plans for those riches. He is not an investment manager giving us great investment advice unless we are submitted to Him and He knows He can entrust us with a wealth of resources. He also wants us to become more of the people He wants us to be. The journey with God is important to God, not how much money we make or how prosperous we become.

I realize that when my focus was on money or power, I always ran into trouble. The mission or plan that God gives me is to start me on my journey of faith and trust. As I look back, I can see He gave me some measure of wisdom, which he continually updated as I followed Him. This kept me on my journey, but the path continually changed. This was true for all the time I was at A-1. Things changed in 2006 to completely reshape God's plan and mission for me. Our son Jason rose to the helm of A-1 so that God could use Diana and I in a different way.

WISDOM IS KNOWING GOD'S PLAN AND MISSION FOR ME: THRIVING THROUGH GOD'S WISDOM

In the later part of 2006, I was already closely connected to Surfing the Nations, a ministry led by Tom and Cindy Bauer. I was on their board, and the ministry was in need of new headquarters since God had led their sponsor church Grace Bible Honolulu to sell their two major properties in the Alewa and Kalihi areas of Honolulu. Surfing the Nations spent the second half of 2006 looking for property that provided housing, warehouse office space, and a place for what Cindy Bauer said was their most important ministry: feeding the hungry. By the end of October, God had provided everything but a place to feed people. We reached out to many known contacts that seemed to have a large area for feeding people as well as parking. By early December, things looked grim.

On December 14, Tom Bauer received a call from architect Russell Ito; he could arrange a meeting to look at a property in lower Kalihi on Kamehameha IV road near School Street. The property belonged to Hawaii Cedar Church, and by December 19, they received approval to use their facilities for feeding those in need. Surfing the Nations announced on December 21, that they would take their normal week off between Christmas and New Year's Day, and they would start serving meals again on, January 4, 2007. Tom said it was a miracle. I say that it was God's normal. God provided just as the clock ran down.

I had been teaching a Bible study for Surfing the Nations on Thursdays at the old Kalihi location. After the move, we had our first meeting in the new church on January 3, 2007. The old meeting location was a small room, livable and cool for surfers, but a fixer-upper. The new location was a church with a rich Korean heritage, a beautiful stage, a sound system, and air conditioning. I remember thinking to myself during that first Bible study, "This is cool."

Over the next few months, God moved me along quickly. I started doing a Bible study for a Hawaii Cedar Church program called "House of Love." Hawaii Cedar Church had and continues to have a heart for the poor, homeless, and struggling. After some time, Pastor Darlene asked me if I could preach for their English congregation on Sunday. I felt God was calling since I had noticed a sign about an English service on the first day that I drove into their parking lot for the Bible study. God prepared me as I thought, "I wonder if God will want to involve me in the English service."

I know God is always working for my good, and I try to watch what He is doing. Most of the time, I plant my feet in the ground, put my brakes on, and lean backwards until He has to push me forward. My belief system for most of my Christian life is if God is in whatever I feel is happening, He will not give up. His thought, program, guidance, message, or correction will grow stronger and stronger over time. I have had many corrections and disciplines over my life, so I tell Him, "Lord if that's you, keep it coming." If it is not Him, I realize whatever I think I want to do or set up goes away after time passes.

If I feel the Lord is guiding me, I usually take baby steps. To paraphrase James 4:13-17, if I say I am going to do something like work in the city, I sin; rather I should say, "I'll do it if the Lord wants me to." When Pastor Darlene approached me, I prayed and thought about it and then committed to speak for three Sundays, the last of which happened to be Easter Sunday, April 8, 2007.

All of my Christian life, I tried to do what I believed the Lord wanted me to do. I preached, and I taught Bible studies. God led me into doing the same thing at the English service for Hawaii Cedar Church. There were no specific commitments of time, energy, or resources so I felt safe, and I continued beyond the three weeks. One day, God challenged me. A couple asked me to marry them. I responded, "I'm not a pastor so I cannot marry you." Soon after that, I no longer saw the couple at church.

A few months later, sitting in an Aloha Ke Akua ministry board meeting, God spoke through Pastor Daniel Kikawa who said, "Eh, Jimmy, you should be a pastor. We can ordain you. We can do that for people that we're connected with that are already in ministry, and you fit." They had done that for Kenny Tomita, a police detective who also had a prayer and healing ministry. Sitting in another meeting with Pastor John Rogers and Pastor Tom Bauer, I mentioned what

Pastor Daniel had said and asked them for their opinion. Without hesitation, both said, "Of course you should."

I prayed a few weeks about becoming a pastor, and God made it clear He wanted me to proceed. I went to see my Senior Pastor Klayton Ko with Pastor John. I had intended to tell him the path I was taking of being ordained by Aloha Ke Akua. At the meeting Pastor Ko asked me if I had considered the Assembly of God Global University's Berean Study credentialing program. In my mind, there were too many books, but Pastor John pulled out one of the books from Pastor Ko's library to show me how thin it was. Then he said, "You can probably pass this without even studying." God sometimes motivates us before we even know that He is doing so.

I left the meeting with Pastor Ko's blessing and the intention of working with Aloha Ke Akua. They required no extra study, no books, no effort, and no cost. As we say in Hawaii, it was a "no brainer." I stopped to visit with Pastor Ernie Chow before I left. Ernie had prayed with me on June 6, 1993, the day I received the Lord. In 1998, he was the first to ask me, "Have you ever thought of becoming a pastor?" I wanted to tell him the good news. As we talked, I told him not to worry because even though I was planning to be ordained by Aloha Ke Akua, my heart would always be with First Assembly of God.

I remembered that Katherine Fujino, who led my dad to the Lord before he died, was from First Assembly of God so I would always have a connection to their churches. As soon as I remembered that, I realized in my spirit that God wanted me to become an Assemblies of God minister, rather than take the easy way. God again led me by presenting me an easy way, knowing He would change my path when I came to my senses. He had my heart so He could be patient with my walk.

As I look back, I realize my dad followed the same principle. He knew I was "all in" at A-1 so even though I was drinking heavily and smoking marijuana during the last year of his life, he would wait for me to come around and would be "all in" behind me. For me, that was *agape* love, and it helped me grow more than any amount of discipline, scolding, or criticizing. When fools do stupid things as I did, they do not know what stupid is. In Hawaiian pidgin, "They donno, what they donno." Common sense does not make sense to someone who is a fool like I was. Only God can heal.

Eventually, I became a credentialed pastor, and that led to our small group becoming a formal church, now called Cedar Assembly of God. Earlier this year as I was driving to a Surfing the Nations function, I heard God tell me, although not audibly, something that Tom Bauer always said. In Tom's early years after he came to the Lord, some told him if he wanted to be a totally devoted to God, he had to give up surfing, which he did. In the early 1990s, God brought Tom back to surfing, and he felt the Lord tell him, "You did not choose to be a surfer; I called you to be a surfer." As I was driving up to Surfing the Nations that night, I felt the Lord tell me, "You did not choose to be a pastor; I called you to be a pastor." I realized that all my life, God was preparing me for my final mission, to be a pastor. My years growing up and working at A-1 were preparation for me. I felt a joy in my heart which touched my eyes.

GOD CALLS JASON TO HIS MISSION: THRIVING BY HEARING FROM GOD

In order for me to be a senior pastor, God needed to promote me from President, to Chief Operating Officer of A-1, and then to Pastor of Cedar Assembly of God. God's plan was for our son Jason to accept God's mission for him, which was to lead A-1. Passing the operations of A-1 to Jason was vital. God had prepared him all his life, but I also needed to hear from God that Jason was His choice and to receive direction concerning the timing of the transition.

Jason first worked at A-1 when he was fourteen, and his first summer project was at Pohakea Point. A long trench needed to be dug on a hillside. I thought it would be good for Jason to learn the business from the ground up. What better way to start than by digging a 150-foot trench, 18 inches wide and 24 inches deep? It was tough, but I felt Jason needed the challenge. After a few days of using a pick and a shovel, Jason came home very excited, "Dad, there's a backhoe on the project. Maybe we can hire the company to dig for us." His brilliance shone, even then. I told him that the hill was dangerous for the backhoe, as it might tip over, and if that happened, we would be in big trouble. He gave a little grunt, and then walked away.

Jason worked as an electrician for our company for eight summers. When Jason graduated from the University of Hawaii with a business degree, he decided to join the family business, something that he, like me, thought he would never do. He became an electrician, eventually running projects, and his last large job was the Navy commissary project. He worked under our foreman and oversaw the Navy exchange building.

After that project he came into the office as a project engineer. He finally had his dream job. All of his life, he dreamed of working in an air-conditioned office, doing what his dad did, just talking to people all day. One day, he came to my office looking a little down. He closed the door and said, "Dad, I don't know if I can do this; this is like school, doing homework all day." Of course, he made the choice to continue. Eventually, he was promoted to a project manager, then vice president of operations, then to president on his thirty-second birthday, the same age that I took over A-1. Diana and I had just turned sixty and were pondering what we might do for God with the next ten years of our lives, while we were still healthy and strong.

Jason needed to accept two significant roles as president, namely, oversight and authority over the company. By late 2009, we realized that Jason was fully committed to the Lord and that we should move towards relinquishing control of the company to him. Planning for taxes necessitated relinquishing control, and God showed us the way through our tax and estate-planning team. Oversight of the company could not take place while Jason was running only field operations. He needed to oversee estimating, which my dad always said was one of the keys to the business. Dad taught me that estimating, field operations, and finances needed to be in balance. Jason needed to take responsibility over all of these areas in order for him to truly learn and grow.

Overseeing all three areas was crucial for Jason's further growth in his relationship with God. If he oversaw only those areas in which he did well, he would not need to depend on God. Although he was involved in estimating and negotiating projects that he was running, oversight of all estimating involved much more. The timing of Jason's transition was not ideal since he was still six to nine months away from overseeing the Hawaii Regional Security Operations Center, which was the largest project in our company's history. The next nine months were crucial, but I felt we needed a War Estimating Head. In October 2009, the United States, including Hawaii, was still reeling from the subprime-mortgage financial collapse and the resulting construction slowdown. Jason rose to the occasion and has never looked back.

Jason had the authority to run the business following the Drucker model under which we had operated for the previous twenty-five years. I told Jason that if he was going to deviate from Drucker, he needed to check with me. The problem with this approach is that no one ever knows when he is deviating until after the fact. Besides restricting creative thinking and over-managing risks, my instructions restricted his dependence on God. He would never be in a situation where he would think, "I must hear from God." Instead, he would just run to me to let me tell him what to do. This created dependence on me as a man and stunted his spiritual growth and relationship with God.

God knew this and orchestrated three situations where Jason came to me and asked me for my thoughts on bidding and securing work, and my advice was the opposite of his thinking. I told Jason, "This is my opinion, but you need to hear from God, and you decide based on your discussion with God." Within a few months, Jason decided contrary to my opinions. As I prayed, I believed God was showing me that I needed to give Jason total authority to run the business the way God would want. He would be solely responsible for hearing from God. In January of 2011, I reviewed the three situations with him and told him that I concluded that God wanted me to give him complete authority to run the business. His first question was, "Dad, can I fire you?" Without hesitation I said, "Yes!" He walked away with a smile. He was God's chosen man and was in the saddle. Now I was free.

IS JESUS ENOUGH? THRIVING BECAUSE JESUS IS ENOUGH

His divine power has given us everything we need for life and godliness through our knowledge of him who called us by his own glory and goodness. Through these he has given us his very great and precious promises, so that through them you may participate in the divine nature and escape the corruption in the world caused by evil desires (2 Peter 1:3-4).

When I first came to the Lord on June 6, 1993, I thought I really loved Jesus. I didn't realize I had to go through a lot more to get to the place where I would one day say, "Jesus is enough for life." A few months prior, Diana and I did one of my favorite things by taking a short vacation to Las Vegas. My group of friends the Safaris loved playing poker. It was one of the glues that held us together. We played for fun, although the game was big enough that wives could be upset on a bad night. My early game was Black Jack, and I had studied the book *Beat the Dealer*. You could win at Black Jack by counting cards, and depending on the number on tens in the deck, you adjusted your bet accordingly. Vegas adjusted by the time I visited, and I did not have fun because they were watching for the card counters.

By the early 1990s, a new game rose in the poker world called Texas Hold 'em. I attacked the game as I did many things: I studied it and became a student, read books on the game about strategy, "tells," how much bluffing was good, and how to manage your money. "James is my name, and money is my game," or so I would tell Diana.

With much anticipation we traveled to Vegas in late March of 1993. For me, it was not just about the money, but it was proving I could win. At the time, the game was not the no-limit Texas Hold 'em that dominates Vegas and television today. Texas Hold 'em was played in smaller denominations: $1-2, $5-$10, $10-20, and $20-40 games. With larger games, the competition is tougher. The first night, I played for eight hours and was down $1,000. I could not sleep as I tried to figure out what I was doing wrong. The second day, I got it and started winning on a consistent basis. I would play for twelve to fourteen hours a day, breaking away for food or to spend a little time with Diana, boasting about my hands, how I played them, and how "007" controlled the table. Diana was gracious and pretended she was interested.

I remember one older man, chubby and balding, who sat on my right one night. When he sat, he carried arrogance in his wad of rolled hundreds that he put on the table. These were table stakes games, and you could only play with money you had on the table. I set my sights on humbling him; it is what James Bond would do. I took pleasure in outplaying him and watching him peel off hundred after hundred. After he lost a good part of his wad, I can still remember his hand shaking as I bluffed him and trapped him as I could. Then something hit me, which is not healthy for a poker player: compassion for him. I felt uneasy, and I felt sorry for him. Did he have family at home? Where was home?

I soon lost one big hand and left the game. It was our last night, yet I considered it mission accomplished for 007, as I knew how to play the game and could win as long as I followed my plan. I came home with approximately $4,000 in winnings and dreamed of playing in bigger games the next time.

These plans were upended in June 1993. God was testing me. He knew I would give my life to him on June 6, 1993. It was written in His book when I was born. Now that I was born again, what would happen to my poker game? The money was not the issue since I had all I needed as a contractor in business for myself. The issue was my way of winning the battle. I was not very good at any sports, but because poker is a thinking man's game, I could at least be competitive and could have my day of glory. When you nail someone with a sneak-attack hand, winning or losing does not matter. What counts is that you caught your opponent off-guard. That is the hand you remember.

Once I came to the Lord, I knew I could not go back to Vegas and play the game. The picture of that older man with his hands shaking lingered in my mind, and I realized I could not please God if I was taking advantage of people. On the other hand, I felt the friendly games at home could continue. I loved playing with the Safaris, and God allowed it. However, I was also playing with a group in the construction industry. It was fun, but I remember one day I felt the Lord tell me I had to give up that game. It was not sinful, and I was not taking advantage of anyone because the game was small and they were all doing well. Yet, the nagging feeling persisted. This was one of my first experiences where something was not bad, but I felt that if I loved God, I just needed to give it up or deny myself the pleasure of enjoying what I loved doing. I needed to decide that I could thrive simply because Jesus is enough.

LESSON FROM DAVEN ON DENYING: THRIVING
THROUGH DENYING

In 1999, I took my sons Jason and Daven to experience world-class surf on the Island of Tavarua in Fiji. We went with a group who booked the island and had been doing so for the previous twelve years.

We landed on the island in the afternoon, and immediately, everyone ran to the tower to check out the surf. "It's going off!" they exclaimed. Everyone jumped into the boat and traveled for thirty minutes, during which you could feel the adrenaline flowing. At "Cloudbreak" surf break, surf was three to five feet high, as measured

Jason surfing in Tavarua

by the Hawaiian method of measuring from the back, not the front, as they measure today. The faces were approximately six to ten feet. Everyone surfed until dark. I stayed in the boat because I knew my limits. On Sunday, the surf came down to two to four feet. Monday was my day of glory since the waves were only two to three feet high.

Daven surfing in Tavarua

On Tuesday, everyone went crazy as the surf rose to four to six feet and stayed consistent with even bigger sets on Wednesday.

The island had two other surf breaks. Directly outside the main headquarters was "Restaurants," which had an extra long wave that peeled to the left. If you caught a good wave from the outside and rode it all the way in, the ride might be one hundred fifty yards. The inside wave was razor sharp as well as the reef on which it broke. During low tide, the outer reef was exposed, and the only thing that kept the water over the reef was the wave that you were riding. This means that if you wiped out, you could "taste seaweed." Those who rode the inside wave felt like the wave would continually close out right in front of them. For me it closed because I was slow, but for Daven, Jason, and the rest, it was an awesome ride.

The other break was called "Rights" because it presented a nice right. The surfers had three surf breaks from which to choose. The group split into two with two surf sessions at Cloudbreak: one in the morning and one in the afternoon. Group 1 might have the early morning session and Group 2 the late morning session. Since each group had only 17 people, and a few didn't surf, the first Cloudbreak session may have had only fourteen surfers on a break that could easily handle thirty to forty surfers. The length of the entire break was approximately two hundred yards with multiple points from which to take off. The average surfer caught probably ten to twenty waves per two-hour session. Everyone was truly "stoked" concerning the quality, size, and consistency of the surf. Throw in Rights and Restaurants, and this was truly an epic surf session for all, especially Jason and Daven. In addition, they enjoyed great food, fishing, no chores, and no studies. For them, the experience was heaven on earth. At the end of the trip, many of those in the group commented that they had just experienced the best surf ever.

When we returned to Hawaii, I noticed that Daven did not surf for the first week. Neither did he surf the next month or couple of months. I thought that he would be so "stoked" on surfing that he would continue chasing waves.

During his high school years, Daven had lived to surf. When he found out that Moanalua High School had established a surf club, he was ecstatic and joined. The day he came home to tell me about the club, he told me, "Dad, we have to practice." I shot back, "Daven, you're not allowed to surf everyday." "I know Dad," he replied, but that didn't stop him from trying to surf everyday. Daven surfed at least two to three times a week, sometimes four. I had previously decided that surfing would be my exercise, so I picked Daven up after school two days a week, and we would head to Kewalos, a local surf spot. I remember one day in particular. It was a Monday or Tuesday following a long swell. The week before, there were waves on the North Shore and good waves for the whole week on the South Shore. On this day, no one was out at Kewalos, and it was two to three feet solid. Daven caught wave after wave and got barreled time and again. As I paddled out and he just got barreled, we would both turn to each other and point our first fingers into the sky, acknowledging God who made the water, the reef, the waves, and orchestrated the day that Daven "owned" the Point.

I was surprised that Daven seemed to have lost his interest in surfing after we came back from Tavarua. I asked him what had happened and why he was not surfing. He responded, "Dad, I cannot surf already." What he meant was that since he had experienced the best, local surf was no longer enjoyable. Now the local surf seemed too windy, too crowded, and too small with too much hassle.

As I think about that today, I realize that God used that experience to guide Daven to a new journey, one in which he would become a pastor with Every Nations Ministries. Daven went from loving, thinking about, and living surfing every minute to loving and living for God twenty-four hours a day, seven days a week. I see nothing wrong with that journey.

"If anyone desires to come after Me, let him deny himself, and take up his cross daily, and follow Me" (Luke 9:23-24, NKJV). When I first became a believer, I read these verses and felt that denying myself was a purely spiritual journey and that if I did that, I would draw closer to Jesus. Now I realize that when Jesus tells us something, He is bringing life to us. Denying is not something we do just to make Jesus happy, but it is something good for us. Denying ourselves actually brings us into a fuller life with joy. As the saying goes, less is more. Paul wrote in Philippians 4:12-13 (NIV), "I know what it is to be in need, and I know what it is to have plenty. I have learned the secret of being content in any and every situation, whether well fed or hungry, whether living in plenty or in want. I can do everything through him who gives me strength."

During my first forty-five years of life, I sought things that would bring me delight and joy. I enjoyed many different kinds of foods. I have a good friend who went to Japan and enjoyed the best and freshest seafood, but when he came back, he had a difficult time adjusting to the regular foods in Hawaii, even food at the best Japanese restaurant. His wife told me that when he came back, he could not eat Japanese food. So it was with Daven.

As I apply this example in light of what Jesus taught, I challenge myself to deny myself certain foods, which helps me practice denying and contentment. As an electrical contractor, God sent me on a mission to take care of my customers, which often meant eating with them. Have you ever been on an eating mission for God? It is hard work. I had lunches at least weekly with customers to develop relationships with them. Often, we would eat at Yanagi Sushi restaurant, which, in my opinion, has the best Japanese food in town. I usually ordered different dishes to share.

After we came back from Tavarua, I decided to practice denying myself the pleasure of eating shrimp tempura. Shrimp tempura is not sinful, nor am I allergic, but I thought I would practice denying myself different pleasures for no other reason than Jesus said so. This did not make me more spiritual, but it did help me develop a small measure of self-control. I also developed in my spiritual walk as I graduated to picking up my cross daily and followed God a little better. However, on New Year's Day, do not get between me and my shrimp tempura. On New Year's Day, I eat six jumbo shrimp tempura. Diana makes a delicious shrimp tempura, although Jason claims he makes it since he fries it. Diana does all the work, but Jason says he is the cook. Like father like son. Some things never change. The way of the family.

This concept of practicing being satisfied with less, whether it is less food, visual pleasure, or excitement, has resulted in my enjoying life more. Maybe Jesus knows something about us that runs counter to our intuition. I remember having my usual salad one Monday following a Saturday night when we had enjoyed dinner with our friends. As I was eating my salad, I realized that I enjoyed the salad just as much as the scallops and appetizers that I had Saturday night. My kids say that for me, since my main diet is vegetarian, anything tastes good. While I eat all kinds of vegetarian foods, normal foods really do taste extra good when I do choose to eat them.

I try to enjoy simple pleasures like looking at trees, rainbows, and sunsets because I delight in the One Who makes the trees grow and Who sends the rainbow. Talking to Him is cool. I hope this can help me thrive when I walk through my disaster, whether economic or otherwise. Jesus did not say this, but I think He could have said, "Eat less, and enjoy more."

DENY YOURSELF: THRIVING THROUGH DENYING YOURSELF

My fellow Safaris club member Paul Tomonari told me once that he was eating a big Costco jar of cashews each month. I was shocked as I thought, "No way can anyone eat a whole jar of cashews in one month." I asked Diana to get one, and it was gone in less than a month. Five months and five jars later, God saved me from my new nutty addiction by blessing me with the bowel problems, so I stopped. Nuts are good for you, but if you cannot control yourself, too many cashews are bad. I found myself driving home, thinking about cashews and taking a small handful soon as I got home. Everyone knows if you take a small amount, you end up reaching in six more times.

Pastor Tom Bauer denied himself French fries and hamburger sandwiches in his early years. Now, he denies himself meats, chicken, dairy, eggs and much more, all for Jesus' sake. When I started eating healthy in the late 1990s, I decided to give up candy and cheese. Today, I still do not eat any chocolate or candy in general. I have become lactose intolerant, and now I do not eat dairy products, which has been a blessing since I do not eat ice cream or other creamy desserts. I realize that just like it was for me with alcohol, once I quit, I do not crave it. My addictive nature has never been able to have just one.

God made us with our senses: sight, touch, taste, hearing, and smell. Our primary senses impact our ability to have joy, determine our happiness, and contribute to our sense of peace. Some have joy when they eat a good meal. Some have happiness when they touch their kids or hear music that reminds them of a person that loved that music. Some feel peace beyond comprehension as they sit looking upon the oceans.

God wired us so that we would delight in our senses, but He never intended our senses to replace Him on the throne. The Bible seems to tell us that it is easy to fail in the battle for control of our senses. God made our senses good and has allowed us to choose whether we will be controlled by our senses. He tells us that we must master our senses, or they will master us. We are prone to crashing (Genesis 4:7, Romans 11:32).

I know the practice of denying myself the good things in life helped me reach for higher spiritual levels. Practice can help us become better stewards of the things He entrusts to us. No one can start playing football in the NFL by relying solely on talent or will. They start with practicing the basics from childhood. It takes thousands of hours, years of development, pushups, running routes, and blocking. Jerry Rice, possibly the greatest wide receiver ever who played for the San Francisco 49ers, developed his skills for catching the football while working with his dad who was a masonry contractor, setting bricks with his hands.

When I came to the Lord in 1993, no one had to convince me that I had many weaknesses and bad habits, or as we say in Hawaii, I had "choke" bad habits. I realized there was no way that I could conquer all of them simultaneously so I started to break them one by one. I felt that if I could have one small victory and solidify that victory over time, I could move on to another challenge later.

Our senses draw us away from being good witnesses. If you love shrimp tempura, and there are only three left on the plate with two people behind you, how many do you take? One? Two? Three? None? There is no right answer. We will not go to hell for taking all three, but can we be good witnesses to our family if we continually take for ourselves rather than denying ourselves? Do we need to be first in line so that we get the best? Do you earn the right if you paid for the food? Do you earn the right if you helped peel all the shrimp and cleaned the whole church or home for the celebration? Imagine having these challenges over just one shrimp.

I try to avoid adoring the face or body of a beautiful woman. There is nothing wrong with a fully clothed woman with a beautiful face, but when does adoration of beauty turn into lust? You may say, "It's just a face." How long do I have to stare at a face before the act becomes wretched? When does working for money to provide for my family turn into loving money? When does loving my kids turn into putting them before God, and when does their education, soccer games, or clothing become first in my heart?

For me, I practice denying myself things that activate my senses: chocolate, shrimp tempura, a beautiful face or figure, money and power. Practice giving whatever makes you cheerful, whether that is $1, $10, or more. The Lord is more pleased when you give $10 cheerfully than when you give $1,000 grudgingly. Practice thinking, "All that we have accomplished you have done for us" (Isaiah 26:12). I am still practicing because there is no such thing as arriving so I just keep walking. My prayer is, "Father, help me practice."

Once I gain some measure of victory in denying myself some of the pleasures of life for Jesus' sake, I think I will be more prepared to pick up my cross and start dying for those that I am called to reach. Naturally, the whole process is not a sequential journey, but a simultaneous one, where I deny myself, carry my cross, and follow Him each and every day.

CARRYING MY CROSS

A man was forced to carry Jesus' cross as He was on His way to be crucified and was so weak that He could not make it on his own. The movie *The Passion of the Christ* depicted what may have really happened to Simon of Cyrene after he realized that he had carried the cross of Jesus Christ the Messiah. He was in awe. Jesus went to the cross and has already completed His work, but He tells us to take up our cross. "Then Jesus said to his disciples, 'If anyone desires to come after Me, let him deny himself, and take up his cross, and follow Me'" (Matthew 16:24, NKJV).

My application of carrying my own cross is much simpler. If there are dishes in the sink when I pass by, I need to wash them. I need to give our dog a bath rather than waiting for my turn to come. If Diana gets upset at me, I need to die to myself and zip my mouth.

I realize that the next level of "taking up my cross" requires concern for others. Self-control that is developed at the "denying myself" level is also essential at this level. A person cannot get into high school without graduating from elementary and middle school. He cannot get into college without graduating from high school. In the same way, a person cannot very easily carry his cross and die for others around him without graduating by denying something simpler first.

Once one is able to practice and develop the ability to deny oneself, his soul finds himself more able to love others enough to "die" for them, at least at simpler levels. Continued practice allows one to thrive during increasingly difficult encounters. Those who think they do not have to develop their spiritual muscles because the Holy Spirit will bless them without even trying are fooling themselves. The Apostle Luke emphasizes that we must practice these habits daily because both denying ourselves and taking up our cross require constant practice. These spiritual disciplines, along with dependence on the Holy Spirit, allow us to reach higher and higher levels.

FOLLOW JESUS: THRIVE BY FOLLOWING JESUS

The highest level is following Jesus in every aspect of life so that we begin to see things through His eyes, hear with His ears, and have His compassion so that what breaks His heart breaks ours. We pray and ask the Father for the things that He wants, rather than the things we want. Our desire is the same as His so we have all that we ask because we ask for the same things for which Jesus would ask. Of course I am dreaming, but since this is my book, I am allowed to dream of how life could be. Reality tells me otherwise, that I have to wait for heaven to reach that point. Yet, I can dream and shoot for perfection. Surely, the more we follow Jesus, the closer we get to becoming like Him, and we will thrive, no matter what the disaster.

MY MISSION: THRIVING THROUGH WALKING OUT MY MISSION

RAISING KIDS WITHOUT LOSING YOUR MIND

It is a miracle that anyone raising kids today can survive with their sanity. All of the conflicting child-rearing methods and philosophies; the assistance and conflicting signals from the educational system; the impact from television, movies, and social media; the pressures that parents put on their kids to succeed and the resulting resistance all work against our and our kids' ability to thrive. Add to those adversities the economic difficulties, and the resultant uncertainties make for a "crash-and-burn" family life.

In my early years growing up in Pauoa Valley, we played at Booth Park. It was my central playground from seven to eleven years of age. I played basketball, baseball, and football after school and on the weekends. I went to the park with my friends, and we joined whatever game was in progress. The only organized games in the 1950s were with the Police Activity League (PAL), and that was too advanced for me. PAL also required money and commitment. Plus, only the talented guys played in leagues.

Football was the most fun and our rules were "Booth Park Rules." In essence, anything goes. We had sidelines and end zones marked by our slippers because our feet were tough. We could run on hot roads without slippers. We could play football with as little as four kids, two on each side: one to center the ball and the quarterback. More could play, and the fun part was there was no structure to the game. Anyone could run with the ball, and anyone could pass the ball. We passed as often as we wanted, forward or backward. We called our craziness "Hawaiian Style." It seems like today we almost raise kids the same way: Hawaiian Style.

My strengths in school lay in math and engineering. I did not like English, history, art, or anything that involved reading. We had to read *Gone with the Wind* in high school, and when I saw the book, I almost had a heart attack. *Cliff Notes* saved me; otherwise I would not have passed English.

I never studied books about raising kids or the psychology of children as we were growing up, nor did I think it was necessary once I got married. Diana was a psychology major, and I figured that was enough. Anyway, those books were too thick with small print and were bad for the eyes. My early concept of raising kids was based on Booth Park Rules. When Jason was six years old, I went into his room one night, and I said, "Jason, you know Dad loves you, right?" He answered, "No." I was a little surprised, but I thought, "What does a six-year-old know?" so I proceeded to tell him my educational philosophy.

"When you become eighteen years old, you will have to move out of the house and take care of yourself. So between now and eighteen, you have to develop your mind, your body and your soul so you are ready. School develops your mind, judo develops your body, and Mom and Dad will help your soul." I noticed that as I was talking, he started to cry, but no loving father with a Booth Park upbringing would stop over a few tears.

I continued, "So it's your responsibility to do your homework, study hard, practice hard at judo, and do all of your one hundred push-ups, sit-ups, bunny hops, etc. I don't want to hear Mom, your teacher, or your judo sensei (instructor) telling me you are complaining about going to judo, not doing your homework, or not doing all of your exercises. If you think you don't need to listen to Mom and Dad's program, you are welcome to move out anytime and take care of yourself." Dr. James Dobson talks about memorable moments, but I do not think he had this talk in mind.

I repeated the same speech to Daven and Lisa after they started school at around six years of age. The good thing about Booth Park rules is that you can change and add new rules to the base as you move through life. I might have been hard on the kids, but judo was a really tough program so I needed to draw a solid line in concrete for their development. Life would be tough on them so it was better that they learned early. Jason went to judo when he was five years old, and judo classes were on Monday, Wednesday, and Friday from 5 to 8 p.m. and on Saturday from 8 a.m. to noon. All of our kids went to judo and soccer, and none of them got into trouble when they were young because they were too tired. The program essentially worked as they did not grumble much to Diana as she got them ready for judo or school or as they worked on their homework.

Jason fell in line, as did Daven and Lisa. Daven was four years younger than Jason, and Lisa was four years younger than Daven. They all grew up living a very rigid, disciplined lifestyle. There was very little grumbling. Diana would say I was not around to hear the grumbling, but they did not grumble when dad got involved. No one wanted to be the first to move out of the house, especially when they were between the ages of six to ten years old.

Jason, Daven, and Lisa

DAD - THE DICTATOR

One significant part of raising our kids was the "super chai." The super chai was a nice whack with the belt—not a beating, but a nice, firm, loving whack on the butt. If the kids got out of line, they would get one super chai when we went home. It was based on a values-oriented discipline. They would earn a super chai for the following: dishonor, disrespect, irresponsibility, a lack of integrity, or a lack of humility. The main focus was on dishonorable and disrespectful actions, especially to Mom or Dad, but even to each other. The kids also could not tattle on each other because that would be a combination of lacking honor and respect for each other: to tattle meant you did not respect your sibling and wanted to get them in trouble and receive a super chai. So we stopped them if they complained about Jason being a bully. I said, "Mom and Dad are with you the whole day. We would be able to see if Jason does something dishonorable, and if he does, he will get his super chai."

In order to teach them these values, we discussed them during dinner. I would ask them to share what they saw that day that was responsible and what was irresponsible, respectful and disrespectful, honorable and dishonorable. We used that model to teach them values, and when they fell out of line: wham, super chai.

I believe that because we had a clear, consistent, measurable method, where the resulting discipline was in the form of scolding or the ultimate super chai. We did not count, "One, two, three." If they did something wrong for which they knew discipline was involved, they earned a super chai. A second offense in the same day resulted in a "super super chai," which was still one whack, only firmer. Let me emphasize, there is no court today for which the level of discipline I gave would be considered child brutality. There were no bruises and never a muscle, tendon, or bone injury, but it stung.

I mention these early years, not as a great method for raising kids, but to emphasize that I believe God was guiding my direction in raising kids. It actually was a good thing that I did not learn any of the new liberal child-raising techniques. We applied good, consistent, old-fashioned discipline that I learned from my mom and dad. Once consistently applied, all three kids actually received very few super chais. Jason had the most, maybe ten to twenty in all, while Daven had maybe six, and Lisa had about the same amount as Daven. Many times I would just take the kids into my bedroom, have them bend over on the bed, make a loud sound with the belt as I snapped it, and I would say, "You know what you did wrong?" "Yes, Dad." "Okay, go!" and they would scoot out of the bedroom with a happy face.

When I got saved in June of 1993, things changed. Jason had just turned seventeen, Daven was twelve, and Lisa was eight. By the end of the year, I realized some of my original methods were not biblical. The main problem was my rule that the children would need to move out and take care of themselves if they did not listen. So in

January 1994, during a family dinner, I told Jason, who was soon to be eighteen, that because the Bible did not teach it, he was not required to move out at eighteen. I can still picture his giant smile of relief as the "move out" law was still on his mind. He loved his room, his bed, his pillow, and his mom's cooking.

The most significant change was control. I realized that I was dominating almost every aspect of their lives. It was similar to the management theory that I had adopted from Peter Drucker: Management by Objective. I had an objective and goal for their lives, and I set out to accomplish these objectives via education, sports, rules, discipline, and programs. When the Bible became my life's guide, my focus shifted from preparing the kids for the tough life ahead to leading them to Christ. I realized only Christ could prepare them for life. Daven and Lisa readily embraced Christianity, although they were not yet "saved." They both said, "Dad, if you say so, we believe." Jason was blinded by evolution and New Age thinking, and he rejected Christ and Christianity in general.

I knew a heavy-handed approach was not biblical, so I set a new course: studying the Bible together. Our kids were still in judo, but Dad had a plan. We were already going to church together, but I wanted us to study the Bible together every night. I let them choose: Jesus or judo. I assumed it would be an easy choice, as our Bible study would be about fifteen minutes, and dinners would not have to be on the run as they were while they were going to judo three times a week. For Daven and Lisa, it was a no brainer; all of a sudden they were very interested in the Bible. On the other hand, Jason, who had been practicing judo for twelve years, surprised me because he wanted to continue judo. He had a chance to be the first athlete to become a judo champion for four consecutive years in the Oahu Interscholastic Association, and we all know what chasing after fame can do for a person's psyche.

RAISING KIDS, GOD'S WAY WITH HAWAIIAN STYLE

It was about this time that I developed another Booth Park concept for raising kids that affected how we raised them. This was to change our philosophy of raising kids so they could freely say, "Dad was a dictator." I truly was, but I know I was a benevolent dictator. Anyone who loves their kids has to be a dictator in some form or another. In fact, Jason is now accused of being a dictator as he raises his daughter. We were so consistent and over-bearing in our method of discipline that it was hard for them, especially Lisa. She would later say, "I would get so angry," about Dad's methods. Outwardly, she appeared to be a good little girl because she complied, but inwardly, there were times, I imagine, where a mini volcano was stirring.

Our new Booth Park concept consisted of the following divisions.

1. From birth to twelve months, kids are "little gods" or rulers; they cry so we fly. During the first few months, crying babies get their way. This is God's way of helping us know their needs. When they cry, they are hungry, need to be changed, or are sick. After about eight to ten months, something interesting happens. The babies learn that they are little gods and can control their parents by crying. This is a trap into which many parents fall of teaching them to be "baby monsters." You see them in malls and grocery stores.

2. From twelve months to twelve years, kids need to learn parents are the gods (rulers) of the house. Parents must raise kids and train them in the way they should go. Parents need to maintain control and not give control away to the babies, or they risk creating baby monsters. They need to teach them and show them how to live in every aspect of life. There is a good way and a bad way. There are good results and bad results.

3. From twelve to eighteen years, we need to turn our kids over to God slowly, say ten to fifteen percent each year, so that by the time they are eighteen, they have a vibrant living relationship with God. Emergencies that happen are opportunities for them to hear from God. This does not mean that we just let them do anything they want. Instead, they must realize there is risk involved in driving late at night, coming home at 2 a.m., etc., and that they will be accountable to God for anything that happens. We as parents will still support them, but they need to start making their own choices within acceptable boundaries. We pray they will grow in their relationship with God and that God protect them out there. I believe this step is crucial, more important than education and sports development, although they play an important role. If we fail to encourage their development of their personal relationship with and dependence on God, they will start their adult life like a little child left alone in a candy store.

4. From eighteen to twenty-two years old, we must turn our kids over to God completely. They are responsible for making their own decisions, although you pray that they come and talk over issues, at least the ones they feel secure in discussing. They should be able to decide most things for themselves. Lisa had a friend who went to Hawaii Baptist Academy for twelve years, did well, and went off to a mainland university. After one year, he wanted to come home. His parents told him, if he did, he would be on his own. They did not spend all that money on private school to let him waste his education. Something is drastically wrong with that picture. They were too controlling.

The general biblical foundational principle for raising kids is that I believe our kids are entrusted to us from God. They are His kids first and foremost, and our job is to raise them. He will cause all things to work together for their good. He loves them. If anything happens, He knows, He allows it, or He orchestrates the situation. Diana and I need to trust Him first as we raise our kids. Too much control of our kids can suffocate their relationship with Jesus. I believe that the teen years are the most critical in their early spiritual growth. These years can be "make or break" as they try to get the first ten to twenty percent of their spiritual foundation solidified. I would not know what is too much or too little control. Only God can guide you there.

I believe for many of us, God looks down at the way we raise our kids, and this is a possible conversation.

God says, "You really don't trust me, do you? If you did, you would trust that I would be watching over your kids in whatever they were doing."

We ask God, "What do we do that justifies You saying that?"

God says, "You want to live with me under grace, but you want your kids to live under law."

We ask God, "Show me a passage that backs up Your statement." God says, "I'm glad you asked. Galatians 3:24-25 says, 'So the law was put in charge to lead us to Christ that we might be justified by faith. Now that faith has come, we are no longer under the supervision of the law.' You expect your growing kids to live under law, and you control their lives by law. They will never learn My grace."

When Lisa was fourteen, she started to come home later and later. One day Diana wanted a meeting, so we sat Lisa down, and Diana said, "Lisa, you are coming home too late, what time should your time limit be?" I thought, "Uh oh." Diana thought midnight was workable. Lisa almost went into shock, making an angry face, or as we say, her "habu" face for *habuteru* or "angry" in Japanese. I asked Lisa whether the kids were drinking or doing any drugs. She said, no one was doing drugs or alcohol. They were usually at someone's house with the parents at home. Diana asked her what kinds of things they were doing. She answered that they were hanging out, watching television, listening to music, and talking story. The conclusion of that meeting was that it would be better for her to sleep over at her friend's house rather than drive home early on Saturday morning at 4 a.m. This was not to be a regular, normal lifestyle, but only occasionally. Lisa was satisfied, Diana grudgingly accepted the solution, and I escaped having two angry women in the house. More importantly, we started turning Lisa over to God by letting her make choices.

On Lisa's sixteenth birthday, I felt it was time to make another significant change for strong-willed Lisa. I believe a parent's idea of giving their kids more freedom is to give them more rope but still have a noose around their kid's neck. So I presented to Lisa at our her family birthday dinner, a rope that was cut signifying that I was taking another leap of faith in turning her over to God, although not completely, but in my mind reaching the seventy percent level. She would be accountable to God one hundred percent, and while numbers were not discussed, all understood the concept.

I believe that our job was to love our kids, regardless of what they did. We did our best to raise them, with godly principles and with Jesus as the center. At some point in time, especially as adults, they need to grow their own relationship with God. Their relationship with God cannot grow if they are only thinking, "What will Mom say? What will Dad allow me to do?" Under that life model, their whole life becomes engrossed in planning, strategizing, pleading, begging with, or even outsmarting their parents to get what they want. There is very little accountability to God, and their relationship with God stagnates, or even diminishes. They need to think, "What does God want? What does His Word say? What choice would He desire for me?" If something goes wrong, God will discipline them. God will protect them. God will do what He needs to do. God will do what only He can do.

Lisa's 16ᵗʰ birthday

WALKING WITH OUR KIDS

There once was a family with the perfect job, the perfect home, no mortgage on their house, and all the food that they needed. They did not need new clothes, they had perfect health, and they had all they needed so there was no need for video games, television, or movies. They even had the perfect provider. However, Adam and Eve were not satisfied with all that they had. Even with all that God gave them, they desired more. They desired something that was probably no different from all that they already had, something that would not taste better. What they desired probably did not look better, and it would not give them better health. They knew what God told them, but they wanted to be able to decide for themselves right and wrong, good and evil. They wanted to be able to make the choice for themselves. They knew God provided all they needed, but there was something in their nature that drove them to eat from the tree from which God commanded them not to eat.

God allowed them to make their choice and, since then, has "bound all men over to disobedience so that He might have mercy on them all" (Romans 11:32). Some might not apply this passage to Adam and Eve's situation. I will not argue the theological timing and point. My point is there is almost no way for our kids to live up to our expectations, at least, the expectations that Christian parents have for them. All men, women, and children have an inner desire, lust, or craving to be proud of themselves and their accomplishments. God made our senses of hearing, taste, touch, smell, and sight, including all the delights our brain and hormones generate, unbelievably awesome, and that is an understatement.

Kids, whether they are twelve months or twenty-one years old, gravitate to pleasure as a means of securing short-term, perceived happiness. Old guys like me, realize that pleasure separated from God is a dead end. We understand that joy and peace come through a relationship with God through Jesus. The young may know this, but as they experience the pleasures of life, the drive in their souls overwhelms their minds, and they are caught in a trap. They do not want to sin so they redefine evil and good with words and embrace the philosophies of the world that help them rationalize.

"It's not wrong, if you don't hurt anyone."

"I am free to make my own choice."

"God will forgive me."

"Tolerance means we should tolerate whatever anyone does. Mom and Dad should be more tolerant; times have changed."

"This is not stealing. They stole from me."

"Everyone is doing it."

"How can it be wrong if it feels so right?"

Eventually they are blinded and become slaves to sin.

Some may argue, "Not my kids: they are filled with the Spirit."

I say, "Great, you raised them well, and God did His work in them early," but for the rest of us, we are not so blessed.

WALKING WITH GRACE

The issue here is not one of dealing with how to out-think and out-talk our kids, but the issue is how to thrive and how to help our kids thrive in spite of the reality that wretchedness reigns. Even the Apostle Paul said, "What a wretched man I am!" (Romans 7:24, NIV). I am not condoning a sinful lifestyle by quoting Paul. He was teaching that the only One Who could rescue us from our wretchedness was Jesus Christ, and if Paul was wretched, we are all wretched. I believe one biblical model for thriving during any disaster, including an economic one, is to live grace. God said in His final instruction to us in Revelation 22:21 (NIV), "The grace of the Lord Jesus be with God's people. Amen."

As we allow our kids to develop and grow in their love for God and their relationship with Christ, they will make huge mistakes along the way. They will take wrong steps, head in wrong directions, do things against our wishes, and cause us hurt and pain. I know that if I allow all their bad choices that do not line up with the Bible or their dishonoring comments and lifestyles to affect me, my love would start to grow cold over time. This evil would be worse than their sin and was prophesied by Jesus (Matthew 24:12). I believe Jesus was teaching that in the last days, due to the increase of wickedness and the influence it would have on our kids, believing parents, as well as Christians in general, would get more and more angry, especially at their believing kids who seem to have "gone berserk" living in the world. Their love would slowly grow cold.

I believe the big test is not whether our kids can keep the commandments and live as believers in every sense of the word, but whether believers can still live with *agape* in everyday life, as their kids, their workers, their bosses, and their leaders live completely wretched lives. I believe this is the path to thriving in the last days. If we can still love, we move a step closer to becoming like Jesus.

BREATH OF FRESH AIR FROM THE PAST

As I look back at my life with my dad, mom, and wife Diana, I notice that I was able to thrive in spite of all my disasters. Here are just some of the disasters I have lived.

1. I almost bankrupted A-1 from 1977 to 1979, singlehandedly.
2. My father died in January 1979, when I was thirty-one years old.
3. I got into two major car accidents in 1981 and 1982 while driving drunk.
4. I lived as an alcoholic, but thought all was good. Numerous times I woke up in the morning, looked up at the ceiling, and thought, "I'm home," but could not remember how I got home.
5. I almost bankrupted A-1 again in 1985.
6. I lived and worked through ten years of economic drought in Hawaii from 1993 to 2003.
7. In 2003, the bank and bonding company were ready to pull the plug on A-1 again. It gave me an eerie feeling, sort of like Groundhog Day.

I got through the disasters because my loved ones believed in me. It was not that they thought everything was fine, but God prepared them to stand steadfastly with me as I went through these disasters. They never judged me, criticized, or yelled *"Baka!"* ("stupid" in Japanese).

As I look back, I can clearly see God connecting an invisible golden thread that He wove through all of these traumatic experiences. God walked with me even before I was saved (John 14:17). He was there through people. Someone was always there walking with me, someone who was almost like the face or presence of God. From 1977 to 1978, my dad provided *agape* love. He did not say anything as I almost dragged the business down. He just kept walking with me. He came to work; he kept the faith and kept bidding for work. He didn't have to say anything. He was dying, and yet, he kept walking, until he could not walk anymore. Even then, he kept walking with me.

In 1985, when A-1 got into trouble again, my mom just kept walking with me. She did not rant, rave, or grumble. She kept walking, sold her house, put money back into the business, and moved to a condo, then did not like condo living so she moved to a house. Through all of the adversity, she just kept walking with me.

God walked with me through Diana. During my crazy years, she kept the faith, kept cooking and cleaning, and loved me like I was still her "007." I learned more about *agape* from Diana, my mom, and my dad than anyone else. They were Jesus in disguise.

During my whole married life, Diana went through all the ups and downs of life. I recognize that God prepared her, but she had to do the walking. She walked to work during the bus strike, and she kept walking with me during all the disasters that I experienced. She never criticized, never looked down on me, and always spoke highly of me, no matter the company, whether she was with general contractor's wives, my parents, our relatives, or church friends. I always overheard tidbits, a little here, a little there, and those uplifting words encouraged me. She walked with me, never against me.

This is a biblical model for thriving during a disaster. We must keep walking with our kids through their difficulties without criticizing everything they do. We must always love, always listen, always support them in some way, finding their need and praying for their need. We must practice acceptance, gentleness, kindness, grace, and mercy. We need to trust God to work out good. Is that possible with our kids today? What if the most important part of raising our kids is not making sure they do not sin? What if it is not trying to prevent them from going through a disaster? What if God gets them through their disasters? What if our job is to love them unconditionally? Would you know what unconditional love looked like for your kids, even your adult ones?

HELP MY KIDS THRIVE AND FIND THEIR MISSION

I think most believers would agree on the following priorities in life.

1. God first
2. Family second
3. Work or ministry third

Our relationship with God is first, and our family is second. In my family, I need to put my wife first and my kids second. I believe God's plan and mission for us should be the foundation for the priorities we hold dear. They are linked together like our cells are linked. They cannot be separated without tearing apart our souls. Let me apply this to myself.

I cannot thrive unless I enter into a relationship with God the Father through Jesus Christ, which is developed by the Holy Spirit. This leads me to God's plan for my life and finding my mission. My relationship with God must also lead me to help my kids find their mission and help them activate the cause that God established in their souls at birth. As a result, I believe that God's view of the family is central to life itself. Through the family, we all discover God's mission and the central cause He has for us.

Jesus tells us that the family is the ultimate blessing. "'I tell you the truth,' Jesus replied, 'no one who has left home or brothers or sisters or mother or father or children or fields for me and the gospel will fail to receive a hundred times as much in this present age (homes, brothers, sisters, mothers, children and fields — and with them, persecutions) and in the age to come, eternal life'" (Mark 10:29-30, NIV).

Notice that we have to put God first, even before family, and as we do, we receive an enriched life with our family and eternal life for our whole family. I catch a glimpse of God's specific mission for me. I do not embrace my family's idiosyncrasies, but I walk with them in their journey.

God has a number of important things He wants us to accomplish.

1. Our relationship with Him needs to grow.
2. We must make our contribution to society, and we must accomplish this through our mission.
3. Most of us will work at some job or own a business.
4. We must also make a contribution to the growth of our families, which is the ultimate mission.

There is more that God wants us to do, but this is where some believers get stymied. God does not have only one plan for us. His plan is multifaceted and multipurpose. His plans impact these areas of our lives, as well as many more. In order to thrive, I believe I am called to walk with my blood family, Diana, Jason, Daven, Lisa, and their families, as well as others with which God has planned for me to walk. My call is different from that of Billy Graham, and yours will be different from mine.

I believe families are an important part of God's ultimate mission for us. I need to walk in my mission, and as I do, I develop my relationship with God. I need to walk with my kids through their missions as we all grow in our relationships with God. The key is continuous walking. As we walk together as a family unit, God works in us to guide us to discover our mission. Family is critical towards this end.

I do not need to control my kids' lives in order to get them to do everything I want them to do in every way I would like to see things done or in my timing. If I try to control my kids, I will be interfering with any signals that God desires to send to them.

Allowing our kids to hear from God, I believe, is part of the blessing in Proverbs 13:22 (NIV), "A good man leaves an inheritance for his children's children…" We know that the ultimate inheritance for our children is spiritual and involves them becoming like Christ. Giving our children a spiritual inheritance involves helping them walk with Christ and helping them train their children to do the same.

This is much more difficult in families where a performance-oriented gospel is taught. Parents train their kids to know what performance level is expected. Parents tell their kids what they should and should not do. If their kids do not perform perfectly, their love grows a little colder each time a new disappointment surfaces.

A commitment to walking with *agape* toward children includes words of wisdom but resolves to eliminate criticism and recognizes that walking with kids is essential especially during difficult periods. Walking with *agape* means the kids are free to hear from God, to make mistakes, and with God as their guide, to make course corrections. Walking with *agape* does not demand perfect living, especially not perfection as filtered through the lens of the parent.

FREEDOM FOR OUR KIDS HELPS ME THRIVE, AND SO WILL THEY

Jason got married in 2006, was promoted to Chief Operating Officer and President of A-1 A-Lectrician in 2008, took over estimating in late 2009, and assumed complete control of the company in 2010. In the past few years, he has made some major decisions affecting different parts of the business. He has chosen which general contractors to pursue. He has chosen which jobs to pursue. He has decided how to reduce our overall administrative and overhead expenses.

Each one of these major decisions has far-reaching implications as they affect our customers, our staff, the attitudes of our people, and the types of projects that we do. For some of these decisions, he has come to me to discuss the choices, while for others he has not.

We live together in the same *ohana*-type house (extended family home), and I have observed and overheard many of their family discussions about raising their daughter Jessica.

Many of these choices and decisions would not have been the ones I would have made, but part of walking with him is giving him the freedom to make choices and decisions, knowing that Diana and I are behind him one hundred percent. If something blows up, he knows we will not walk away saying or thinking, "You are on your own. I told you so. Didn't I tell you not to do that? Now it's your problem." Our hearts are united in our walk together trying to follow Jesus, but Jason's issues and struggles are not for us to decide. Therefore, our journey with Jason is never conditional and is not based on my previous input or on Jason's choices. We desire to commit to walking until we cannot walk. My dad did that with me. Jesus walked with His disciples and still walks with us.

Daven and Lisa have similar schedules: they are jammed. Daven and his wife Charity are in full time ministry, and Lisa is building her publishing empire. We have our weekly family Bible study dinner, where the focus of the discussion is, "How have you seen God's hand this past week in your life?" Diana and I are concerned for them in many areas of life including the following.

- Focus of ministry
- Wisdom in spending of their time and resources
- Not making it to family Bible studies
- Where they go that caused them not to make it to family Bible study
- Raising Madison our granddaughter

- Choice of friends
- Growth and development
- Physical, spiritual, and emotional health

I realize that good, sound advice is probably overrated, especially coming from Dad. Walking with my kids through life is not overrated, but it is definitely difficult. I must trust that Jesus knows difficulties better than I.

For us, thriving is not success or all things going well. Thriving is a commitment to walking with our kids, and we hope that we can successfully walk with them, giving them freedom to develop in their relationship with Jesus. He will activate in their souls the cause He has stored in them, will guide them to their mission, and will develop them fully from that point.

6

MY MISSION: THRIVING THROUGH WALKING OUT MY MISSION IN BUSINESS

WALK WITH ME AS I WALK WITH YOU THROUGH THIS BOOK

I joined my dad at A-1 in 1970. Since then, I had dreams of doing something great in business. I now realize that only God does great things, and that realization has set me free from my previous foolishness. Sometimes God uses our minds, hands, feet, or prayers to do great things. Sometimes He uses our connections as we bring people to Him. This includes family, friends, businessmen, fellow workers, and even strangers.

I have studied business principles, concepts, and strategies since the early 1970s, as I tried to make a living and tried to excel. I have tried to keep up with the signs of the times, and I have tried to figure out how to gain an edge and how to figure out the future.

When I finally realized that God knows the future and knows how to prosper a business financially and that all I had to do was give the business to Him, I was set free from striving. It is not that

He will just shower financial blessings on us, but He is in control of all wealth. I find this intriguing. I am not trying to imply that I have figured out God. I cannot induce Him to bless me. I realize God is sovereign, and He alone decides all things. He can bless the wicked, and take away from believers who follow, love, and honor Him. King David was bummed by this. "When I tried to understand all this [the wicked doing well while he suffered], it was oppressive to me till I entered the sanctuary of God; then I understood their final destiny." (Psalm 73:16-17). Like King David, I will leave the global planning to God. He does not favor me above you, and I do not possess any supernatural wisdom from God.

However, I believe that God has hidden gems in His Word about how business people can prosper and thrive during economic disasters. He also tells us that He can give wisdom and wealth to whom He pleases. I cannot wrap my mind around this, but I accept that as truth.

> To the man who pleases him, God gives wisdom, knowledge and happiness, but to the sinner he gives the task of gathering and storing up wealth to hand it over to the one who pleases God... (Ecclesiastes 2:26).

> You may say to yourself, "My power and the strength of my hands have produced this wealth for me." But remember the Lord your God, for it is he who gives you the ability to produce wealth... (Deuteronomy 8:17-18).

I cannot comprehend how God causes us to prosper, but one secret is found in 1 Chronicles 28, which we already covered, but is worth repeating.

> Then David gave his son Solomon the plans for the portico of the temple, its buildings, its storerooms, its upper parts, its inner rooms and the place of atonement. He gave him

the plans of all that the Spirit had put in his mind for the courts of the temple of the Lord and all the surrounding rooms, for the treasuries of the temple of God and for the treasuries for the dedicated things. "All this,'" David said, "I have in writing from the hand of the Lord upon me, and he gave me understanding in all the details of the plan" (1 Chronicles 28:11-12, 19, emphasis my own).

God downloaded the plans for the temple into David's brain, via the Holy Spirit. The same scenario has happened to architect Francis Oda a number of times over his life. God downloaded ideas for designs and plans for traffic solutions and whole communities. Francis has even had visions unfold about the future of Hawaii and the world while in the presence of other people. I hope one day he will write a book to share his experiences, so I will not use any of his material.

What I share is what I have learned, but remember, God is sovereign. I cannot pass on to you the supernatural key to wisdom in your business. Even if you follow the principles that I share, you are not guaranteed business success.

This chapter covers business and financial prosperity, although we all understand that this is only a small part of life since eternal and spiritual blessings trump financial gains. However, finances have always been an important part of the kingdom so I will spend this chapter developing more principles that I learned from God through the Bible and my own life experiences. The key to financial prosperity can be learned from Las Vegas' new hot game, Texas Hold 'em: do not lose it all on one hand.

Here are a few additional tips.

1. Do not let the banks defeat you.
2. Save a little.
3. Reduce consumption because more is not better.

HOW BAD CAN IT GET?
ISN'T SOMEONE DRIVING THE SHIP?

The passengers on the RMS *Titanic* were sure that nothing could happen on their trip. They had faith in the size of the ship, its captain, the eight hundred crew members, and the fact that they were a part of history as they sailed on the maiden voyage. If they were able to step forward into time three months and look back, how many would have still gone on that voyage? How many would have paid all they had for that look into the future? How many would have given all they had for a chance to change their decisions as they purchased their tickets or stepped onto the decks of the *Titanic*?

I believe it is possible that many today will look back three or five years from now and say the following.

"I wish I had done things differently."

"I wish I had planned better."

"I wish I had been concerned with the return of my money rather than the return on my money."

"I wish I had prepared my family for this disaster."

"I wish I had not depended purely on prayer."

"I wish I had not depended on God bailing me out."

WHAT TIME IS IT?

God establishes a principle in His Word about time.
There is a time for everything,
and a season for every activity under heaven:
a time to be born and a time to die,
a time to plant and a time to uproot,
a time to kill and a time to heal,
a time to tear down and a time to build...
(Ecclesiastes 3:1-3).

Solomon is writing a truth from God: cycles cannot be broken. Some are obvious and we do not even think about them, like the rising and setting of the sun. We have the air and water cycles of purification, planting and harvesting cycles, the salmon and monarch butterfly cycles, the spring, summer, fall, and winter cycles, and many more.

In the economy, there are economic cycles that go back to the beginning of human history. Some of these early cycles are tied to the rain cycle, but there are other measurable cycles that affect the economy and the financial markets. There are long-term super cycles such as the Kondratieff Cycle, which lasts about forty to sixty years, as well as shorter cycles of twenty, ten, or five years. There are just as many business theories that attempt to explain the causes of these cycles and how to best help to manage economies once these cycles are recognized.

John Maynard Keynes was the founder of Keynesian economics and presented his ideas in his book *The General Theory of Employment, Interest and Money*. According to Keynesian economists, "private sector decisions sometimes lead to inefficient macroeconomic outcomes which require active policy responses by the public sector, in particular, monetary policy actions by the central bank and fiscal policy actions by the government to stabilize output over the business cycle."[1] Although what Keynes states is true, the nature of government is to overreact as it tries to "stabilize output over the business cycle." Those in government may mean well, but as they try to balance the economy, they may violate God's principles. This may result in a larger *Titanic*-sized disaster for the whole world. What if the "inefficient macroeconomic outcomes" are just what our world needs so that people do not take hyper-speculative risks, thinking that the government will rescue them?

The Austrian business cycle theory put forth by Nobel Prize winner Friedrich Hayek, explains the current business cycle this way:

"The theory views business cycles as the inevitable consequence of excessive growth in bank credit, exacerbated by inherently damaging and ineffective central bank policies, which cause interest rates to remain too low for too long, resulting in excessive credit creation, speculative economic bubbles, and lowered savings."[2] In Hawaiian, if you create too much money for everyone, the SH_T will hit the fan at some point in time.

I believe neither the Keynesian or Austrian theory would matter if God were running the economy. Since that is not the case, I will offer my opinion as to which theory has governed the United States and the world, and which, if either, has an explanation for where we are today.

EXTREME LEVELS OF CREDIT CREATION

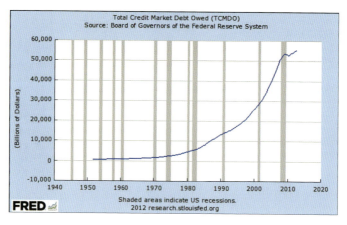

The following two charts help us understand the current United States debt situation.

The Total Credit Market Debt Owed chart shows the total debt owed by all sectors of the United States at approximately $55 trillion as of 2012.

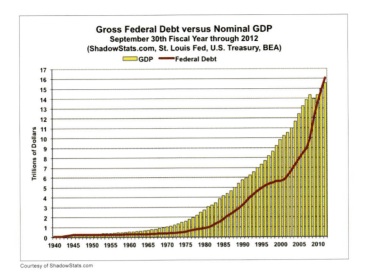

Courtesy of ShadowStats.com

The second chart shows the US federal debt plotted against the Gross Domestic Product (GDP). In 2012, the GDP was approximately $15.5 trillion. Thus, the total debt to GDP ratio is approximately 350%.

I would argue that the increasing federal debt has less of an impact on the GDP. The federal government spent money and increased its debt but has not had a positive impact on the US economy as it might have had in the past.

From 1980 to 1990, the federal debt increased by approximately $2.3 trillion, while the GDP increased by approximately $3.1 trillion, yielding a ratio of 1.3. From 1990 to 2000, the federal debt increased by approximately $2.4 trillion, while the GDP increased by approximately $4.3 trillion, resulting in a ratio of 1.8. From 2000 to 2010, the federal debt increased by about $7.0 trillion, and the GDP increased only $4.7 trillion, which yielded a ratio of only 0.7.[3,4]

The debt-GDP situation is like stepping on the gas while driving, only to have the car slow down. Something is wrong with the car, just as something is amiss with the economy. The federal government is pouring more money into the economy in an effort to keep it going.

The government has increased its disruption of the normal ebb and flow of the economy. Without addressing whether the reasons for disruption are justified or whether the involvement is too liberal or too conservative, I believe that the amount of total debt that exists within the US economic system, as well as the world system, is fast approaching, or may have already exceeded, the point at which the world governments are in control of the fix. Governments are forced to continue to push money into the economy in order to prevent a major calamity. Governments know that ceasing to feed the economy would be disastrous, but they do not know what will happen as they continue to pour more money into the economy. So the game continues as they kick the can down the road.

The danger is that with each kick, the potential for a sudden cyclical "regression to the mean" is greatly increased. God's biblical principle of cycles is such that a sudden disastrous correction could take place very quickly. This does not mean the world is coming to an end, but many may experience a great deal of intense pain. Two

Kicking the Can Down the Road

groups that may be hurt the most are the American middle-class and Americans with debt.

The American middle-class, including those who are above the poverty line but live day-to-day, will be adversely affected by an economic crisis. These people have seen their real income levels as well as total wealth slowly diminish over the past twenty years and have very little savings today. They have succumbed to debt in order to sustain their standards of living. The falling dollar has made things more expensive. Two things can happen that will increase the pain very quickly for them.

1. The dollar value has already fallen about 35% against a group of currencies and could fall much further and much quicker. China has eased the pain from the 35% fall of the dollar by selling cheap goods, which has helped America and the world to seemingly thrive. That door will soon close, as China will start to have its own economic problems when the world's economic situation reaches a crisis point. The US is in trou-

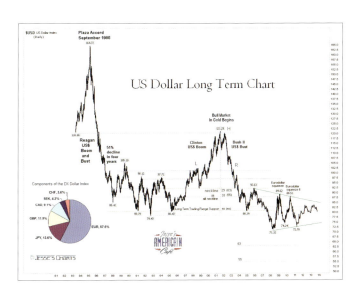

ble if the dollar falls 10% in six months and is in dire straights if the dollar falls 20% in six months.

2. The dollar could lose its status as the world's reserve currency. Right now, any major purchase made in the world is settled in dollars. If a country buys oil, it is quoted in dollars, and the buyer must pay in dollars. This has kept the dollar as the major reserve currency as all countries are holding dollars in cash (mainly electronically), or government treasury bills (short term instruments), notes (two- to five-year instruments), or bonds (ten- to thirty-year instruments). If the dollar were no longer the world reserve currency, and I believe this is coming, Americans would immediately see the value of their financial portfolios dramatically decrease and the cost of all goods dramatically increase.

Americans and businesses with debt that needs to be refinanced by banks will be affected by a world economic crash. Anyone that owes debt to banks, any financial institutions, or businesses, might see a call for repayment upon any new refinancing. They might also see more stringent loan requirements, like those of the past four years. This will take place at the same time that personal finances are stressed. This might be caused by the regression to the means scenario, where the total credit starts shrinking. Imagine if the total credit were to reduce from $54 trillion to $50 trillion to $45 trillion over a period of one to two years. This reduction would cause much pain for borrowers. What might cause the reduction in credit? A halt in refinancing of the United States government securities by the United States and major sovereign governments would cause a reduction in total credit. No one will buy US bonds and notes.

At present, US banks are a major source of financing for government securities. If there was a run on the banks for cash, and banks are holding US government securities that cannot be resold for cash, the banks would depend on the US government for cash. However, external

forces may severely limit the US goverment. The US and world economies are complicated.

ECONOMIC EXPLANATION ACCORDING
TO KEYNES AND HAYEK

The American government has tried to do its best to help Americans.
However, the American government economists have followed
Keynesian economics, and in the years after World War II, this model worked well. Around the early 1990s, the economists in control,
had good intentions, attempted to keep the economy progressing,
and continued to prevent even a small measure of pain caused by
severe recessions. In order to prevent recessions, economists inflated
the fiscal and monetary support systems. Each time a mini disaster
unfolded, the government opened the pumps, and politics may have
played a role.

According to Hayek and the Austrian business cycle theory,
priming the pumps with money would eventually lead to excessive
growth in bank credit, bad central bank policies, low interest rates,
extreme and excessive credit creation, speculative economic bubbles,
and lowered savings. This is exactly what is happening now. Keep in
mind, Hayek's work was written in the early 1970s.

The US government has followed Keynes policies but has now
entered a potential disaster zone, according to Hayek. The situation
would be interesting if it was not so dire. The situation has been made
tenfold worse because America is not the only one affected by the
creation of excessive credit. Now, the whole world is in trouble. Most
Americans have been desensitized to the seriousness of the situation.
They see what people saw on the decks of the *Titanic*: a captain at the
helm, hundreds of engineers, hundreds of deck crews, hundreds serving in the cabins, dining rooms, and recreational areas. The *Titanic*
had steel plates three-quarters of an inch thick and was almost three
football fields in length. What did they have to worry about?

Americans today think America is unsinkable. We saved the world during World War I, World War II, and the Korean War, and we stood strong so that the Soviet Union crumbled and the Iron Curtain fell. America has had the strongest economy in the world for the past sixty years and has the largest stock market. The American dollar is the reserve currency of the world. We are the greatest country that has ever lived, bar none. We think nothing can happen to us.

I must emphasize that I love America. My dad served in the 100th Battalion, 442nd Infantry. He served and was ready to die because he loved America. He served so his kids could have a future in this great country. However, it is foolishness to drive one hundred miles an hour on a road covered with fog and ice. America is now covered with fog and ice, and we are in dangerous territory. Those driving cannot see clearly and cannot stop even if they want to stop. We may have passed the point of no return.

IS THERE AN ECONOMIC EARTHQUAKE HERE?

DREAMS

The Bible tells us that in the last days, "young men will see visions, old men will dream dreams" (Acts 2:17). All the dreams in the Bible were from God and were His means of communicating to the people in Old Testament times, but they are also for us, as these dreams teach us that God communicates to people. Not all dreams were given to God's chosen people, the Jews; God gave dreams to many gentile kings.

With that in mind, I want to share a trio of dreams that I experienced in early 2008. First, let me explain what I believe is a biblical truth. God is the sender of dreams. All dreams in biblical stories include dreams sent from God. God knows all things and proves that He does by what we call a déjà vu experience.

A déjà vu experience is when you experience something, and you feel like you have been there or seen the scene, even though you know you have never been there or seen the particular scene previously. I believe our déjà vu experiences show us that God is revealing our future to us. He has a giant iPhone, takes a picture of a scene that does not yet exist, and then downloads the scene into your soul or brain. God has been wooing us all along, proving to us that He knows everything, and proving to us that He is truly omniscient. It is as if He has been jumping up and down around us, in front of us, in our dreams, and in our visions, calling to us, "Here I am; follow me."

I try to write down my dreams, especially the ones that may seem to teach me something. Here are my three dreams.

DREAM #1 ON JANUARY 7, 2008

I was on a mountaintop ridge, maybe one hundred feet up, in a concrete building or bunker. I felt like something was coming from the ocean. Horses were moving away from the beach. People were mulling around on the beach. Eventually, the tide started retreating, so in the dream I knew a tidal wave was coming. I wrote the following interpretation in my notebook: "Economic Tidal Wave?"

DREAM #2 ON FEBRUARY 20, 2008

Part 1: I was at a beach that looked like Kewalos at Ala Moana, watching the eight- to ten-foot large surf and a boat as it was towed in with a girl and guy hanging onto the front of the boat.

Part 2: There was a big sand hole at the beach that felt like Ehukai. The surf was high, and there was a baby in the hole. A wave came through a cave-like structure in the ocean, just off-shore. The wave engulfed the baby, who disappeared, but the baby's dad came to the rescue. After the wave receded, the father left the baby. The next wave came pushing a big surfboard through the sand hole, but the baby was not there. I wrote this interpretation in my notebook: "I need to help people." I did not connect this dream to Dream #1 at this point.

DREAM #3 ON JANUARY 27, 2008

I was surfing, I see a 50' wave coming. I was paddling on a body board, trying to get out. The wave did not break, but I paddled over it, thinking I would wait for a good wave. The water was shallow because my fins touched the reef.

Eventually, I tied the three dreams together and thought, "An economic tidal wave is coming," which I wrote in my dream journal next to my notes from the dream I experienced on January 7, 2008. For me, it was God making clear what was coming.

As a result of these three dreams, we revisited our "Joseph Plan." I had gone through two periods where we were almost bankrupted (1978-79 and 1984-85) and had experienced a long recession that impacted the construction industry from the late 1990s to 2003. Although we still had a decent number of projects in our pipeline and the market was still strong, I realized that God was revealing what was coming so that we could prepare. Accordingly, we reinstated our Joseph Plan preparations.

Our Joseph Plan was based on the lesson God gave us in Genesis 37-50. In essence, Joseph became second in command to the Pharaoh of Egypt. God sent Pharaoh two dreams about the future. The dreams troubled Pharaoh; I think they were nightmares to Pharaoh. Joseph interpreted the dreams for Pharaoh and told him Egypt would have seven years of great abundance followed by seven years of famine.

Eventually Pharaoh put Joseph in charge of all Egypt, second only to himself. Joseph's plan for Egypt's survival was to save one-fifth of all grain harvested during the seven years of abundance, and that food was to be held in reserve to be used during the seven years of famine, "so that the country may not be ruined by the famine" (Genesis 41:36). I believe this is a biblical model that can be followed for any difficult period, so at A-1 we followed it during the late 1990s and felt it should be implemented again. In Pidgin, "No eat all. Save something for tomorrow."

HAS AMERICA SOLVED THE PROBLEM?

The big question at hand is whether the economic quagmire that took place from 2008 to 2009 is over or not. I believe that the underlying structural problems have gotten worse and that the governments of the world have essentially gone "all in" to try to solve the underlying problem of carrying too much credit and debt by carrying more credit and debt. It is like giving a heroin addict methadone and heroine to try to help him. Of course, whether you can see what is happening depends on your lenses. Your lenses are your foundational economic model, which determines whether you are able to understand the times and clearly see what is taking place.

Those in power in America and the world have followed some form of Keynesian type cyclical programs. They poured money into the private sector when it got out of balance and started to contract. They thought any level of pain for our society was bad. When they first started out fifty or sixty years ago, and until recently, they may have had options and choices. Today, they have no option but to continue what they have been doing, except now exponentially greater amounts of money are required. A trillion dollars are needed here, another trillion dollars are needed there, and before you know it, trillions of dollars are needed everywhere.

Those from the Austrian School of economic thought can see and understand the magnitude of the problem. They are not smarter, but they can see clearer, because they have a business model that understands cycles and clearly aligns with what the world powers have been doing for the last twenty to thirty years. What started with excessive bank credit for businesses has led to speculation in all types of investments: stocks, real estate, credit default swaps, mortgage back obligations, and financial derivatives that no one truly understands. Bad central bank policies, low interest rates, extreme and excessive credit creation, speculative economic bubbles and lowered savings have resulted. Worst of all, the sovereign governments of the world today are in the deepest financial, economical, and social turmoil since the Great Depression. This is exactly what the Austrian School anticipated would happen. The powers in control, including US Federal Reserve Chairman Ben Bernanke and friends, know something is wrong, and they think they can fix the problem. They think America can bail out Europe. They may be making things worse so that the ultimate fall becomes humongous.

CAN ANYONE EXPECT THE UNEXPECTED?

There is something very unusual about disaster: everyone knows it could happen, but almost no one expects it to happen today or tomorrow. If every tomorrow becomes a today, should we not anticipate and be ready for the unexpected disaster today? There are a number of extremely insightful writers that have books on different aspects of this idea. I will briefly cover three of them.

THE BLACK SWAN BY NASSIM NICHOLAS TALEB

This book discusses "The Impact of the Highly Improbable." Dr. Taleb presents an interesting thought: people originally thought all swans were white. No one thought black swans existed until they saw the first black swan. He then brands the concept of the "Black Swan" as an event with three attributes.

"First, it is an outlier, as it lies outside the realm of regular expectations, because nothing in the past can convincingly point to its possibility.

Second, it carries an extreme impact (unlike the bird).

Third, in spite of its outlier status, human nature makes us concoct explanations for its occurrence after the fact, making it explainable and predictable."[5]

"Black Swan logic makes what you don't know far more relevant than what you do know."[6]

"Our inability to predict in environments subjected to the Black Swan, coupled with the general lack of the awareness of this state of affairs, means that certain professionals, while believing they are experts, are in fact not."[7]

One example he uses is the Maginot Line. "The French, after the Great War (WWI) built a wall along the previous German invasion route to prevent reinvasion-Hitler just (almost effortlessly) went around it."[8]

"History is opaque... the human mind suffers from three ailments as it comes into contact with history, what I call the triplet of opacity:

1) The illusion of understanding, or how everyone thinks he know what is going on in a world that is more complicated (or random) than they realize;

2) The retrospective distortion, or how we can assess matters only after the fact...

3) The overvaluation of factual information and the handicap of authoritative and learned people..."[9]

My application of the Black Swan theory put forth by Nassim Taleb is that no one expects a potential economic disaster and no one can predict it. What people know actually works against their recognition of the disaster. Experts, the powers in control, are actually blinded by the Black Swan event when it occurs, and the eventual impact is much greater than anyone could imagine.

UBIQUITY BY MARK BUCHANAN

This book attempts to explain "Why Catastrophes Happen." The definition of ubiquity is "present, appearing, or found everywhere."[10]

Mark Buchanan brings forth a new idea (not new to God), "out-of-equilibrium physics."[11] This gives us a clue to the cause of upheaval. "The key is the notion of the critical state, a special kind of organization characterized by a tendency toward sudden and tumultuous changes, an organization that seems to arise naturally under diverse conditions when a system gets pushed away from equilibrium."[12] In Hawaiian pidgin, "If something's out of balance, it's gonna blow."

"Chapter One-Causa Prima" starts off as follows. "It was 11 am on a fine summer morning in Sarajevo, June 28, 1914, when the driver of an automobile carrying two passengers made a wrong turn… pulling into a narrow passageway with no escape. The automobile stopped directly in front of a nineteen-year-old Bosnian Serb student, Gavrilo Princip. A member of the Serbian terrorist organization Black Hand, Princip couldn't believe his luck. Striding forward, he reached the carriage. He drew a small pistol… pointed ii. Pulled the trigger twice. Within thrity minutes, the Austro-Hungarian Archduke Franz Ferdinand and his wife Sophie, were dead…"[13] These events triggered World War I. No one could have predicted this catastrophic turn of events leading to mankind's worst war up to that point in time. Subsequently, World War I became a prelude to World War II.

Chapter 12 makes a statement that might well summarize the point of the book: "If the smallest of details continually intrude on the larger picture, with the power to alter it radically, how is the historian to make sense of anything? Faced with this dilemma, it becomes doubly difficult for the historian to separate the significant historical facts from the background of all facts."[14]

The final two sentences of Chapter 12 state, "It does not seem normal and lawlike for long periods of calm to be suddenly and sporadically shattered by cataclysm, and yet it is. This is, it seems, the ubiquitous character of the world."[15]

I apply Mark Buchanan's concepts to a potential economic disaster, concluding that when an economy (system) gets "pushed away from equilibrium," correction is "sudden and tumultuous."[16] Also, small events can trigger large disasters.

STABILIZING AN UNSTABLE ECONOMY
BY HYMAN MINSKY

Hyman Minsky was an economist that presented economic thinking twenty-five years ahead of his time. It is easier to see clearly once an economic disaster unfolds. Explaining the causes of that disaster is much more difficult. A near impossibility is to explain what will happen twenty-five years before it happens, while also presenting the causes along with the theory. Minsky has done that, and "Minsky moment" is named after him.

Previously, I was not a student of Minsky, but I am intrigued by his thoughts and analysis which seem obvious today, if you can understand the current times without being blinded by the financial media and the powers in control, who will do all they can to prevent you from understanding the underlying problems that exist. They would be blamed if everyone understood. The current summary comes from one of the great impartial financial writers today, John Mauldin, whose newsletters are under the banner of Mauldin Economics and his website http://www.mauldineconomics.com.

Here is a brief summary of the article "Economic Singularity" from Mauldin's website. I quote many excerpts from this article, as Mauldin is a lot smarter than I am.

Hyman Minsky, one of the greatest economists of the last century, saw debt in three forms: hedge, speculative, and Ponzi. Roughly speaking, to Minsky, **hedge financing occurred when the profits from purchased assets were used to pay back the loan, speculative finance occurred when profits from the asset simply maintained the debt service and the loan had to be rolled over**, and Ponzi finance required the selling of the asset at an ever higher price in order to make a profit.

Minsky maintained that if hedge financing dominated, then the economy might well be an equilibrium-seeking, well-contained system. On the other hand, the greater the weight of speculative and Ponzi finance, the greater the likelihood that the economy would be what he called a **deviation-amplifying system**.

A business-cycle recession can respond to monetary and fiscal policy in a more or less normal fashion; but if you are at the event horizon of a collapsing debt black hole, monetary and fiscal policy will no longer work the way they have in the past or in a manner that the models would predict.

While deficit spending can help bridge a national economy through a recession, normal business growth must eventually take over if the country is to prosper. Keynesian theory prescribed deficit spending during times of business recessions and the accumulation of surpluses during good times, in order to be able to pay down debts that would inevitably accrue down the road. **The problem is that the model developed by Keynesian theory begins to break down as we near the event horizon of a black hole of debt.**

Deficit spending can be a useful tool in countries with a central bank, such as the US. But at what point does borrowing from the future (and our children) constitute a failure to deal with our own lack of political will in regards to our spending and taxation policies? There is a difference, as I think Hyman Minsky would point out, between borrowing money for infrastructure spending that will benefit our children and borrowing money to spend on ourselves today, with no future benefit.[17]

As related to a potential economic disaster, Minsky's concepts can be summarized as follows. Speculative financing and investments can lead to an increasingly unstable economy. In a normal business cycle, Keynesian monetary and fiscal policy works. But when an economy reaches what John Mauldin calls a "collapsing debt black hole," these policies cease to work. Unless you return to true growth, rather than speculative credit-pushed growth, prosperity will not return.

Let me summarize some key points pulling the thoughts of the three authors and Mauldin together.

LESSONS FROM NASSIM TALEB

Dr. Taleb tells us we know less than we think we do. The powers in control trying to solve the problem or at least keep the disaster at bay think they know what they need to do.

What we do not know is more important than what we know.

A Black Swan event lies outside the realm of regular expectations, as people have no historical reference for the event. Economists today are looking to history to guide their decisions for tomorrow. That is like driving sixty miles an hour by looking in the rear view mirror.

Black Swan events cannot be predicted, and no one is an expert, although everyone thinks they are as they plunge forward accordingly.

LESSONS FROM MARK BUCHANAN

Dr. Buchanan tells us that small events can trigger huge cataclysmic events that affect everything. Historians cannot look to history to guide them in a financial crisis as they will not know which historical fact, and therefore, which solution, is relevant to solving or ending the current crisis.

LESSONS FROM HYMAN MINSKY

Dr. Minsky essentially teaches that good times will cause people to take larger and more speculative risks, which cause borrowers to move from hedge to speculative to Ponzi finance and that eventually leads to debt accumulation when profits can no longer repay the loan. The only solution is to refinance again and again, each time increasing the amount of debt. What started out as well supported hedge loans that were self-sustaining, in that the assets could generate enough profits to repay the loans, eventually progresses to speculative and Ponzi loans during boom times when loans are made only to speculate on assets, with the hope that these assets appreciate in value enough to repay the loan when the assets are sold.

In America, the economic situation was bad enough when just businesses were involved in the dangerous levels of speculation and Ponzi finance. In the past fifteen years, banks and big financial firms, like Goldman Sachs and Morgan Stanley, have become involved in speculative and Ponzi finance. The big danger is the level with which these firms were able to use leverage: twenty years ago, ten times net worth was normal. In the past few years, leverage has grown to forty to fifty times net worth or more. Naturally, the big boys made a lot of money and took huge bonuses, but when you leverage 50 to 1, you lose everything if the market goes against you 2%. This is why the central banks and the treasuries of the world governments were forced to go "all in" to save the banking system, not to mention relax all the historic rules of prudence.

When the Financial Accounting Standards Board (FASB) was about to issue rulings so that banks and financial firms would have to write down their Level III assets, the powers in control realized that if this happened, most of the major financial institutions would be broke. So they changed the rules, and the game continues. The problems are still growing bigger and worse, as the US Federal Reserve continues to act as a lender of last resort. This situation alone would be dire enough, but now the Federal Reserve is acting as a lender of last resort to the European Central Bank, the European governments, and the whole European system, even while it is teetering on the brink of disaster.

If Taleb, Buchanan, and Minsky were all in the same room together, I can imagine the discussion they might have. Taleb would say, "I think we have a number of Black Swan Events on the Horizon."

Buchanan would ask, "How would you define a Black Swan event?"

Taleb would say, "A Black Swan event is a major economic disaster where the stock market and the bond market collapse fifty percent in one week, and that triggers major bank holidays."
Buchanan would inquire, "What might trigger this Black Swan event?"

Taleb would respond, "Any of the following occurrences could trigger a Black Swan event. A smaller country refuses to take payment in US dollars. A major country refuses to refinance their portfolio of US bonds. Germany pulls out of the European Common Market. Greece refuses to make more fiscal cuts. French workers refuse to reduce their vacation time from six weeks to three weeks. China gets mad and does something crazy to the financial markets. Masses riot in the streets over the lack of food for ten million people in twenty-five nations."

If Minsky were alive, he might close the discussion by saying, "Looks like we are fast approaching the 'Minsky Moment.' I am appalled." Taleb would counter, "I prefer to call it a 'Black Swan,'" while Buchanan would counter, "Sounds like a 'ubiquitous' event to me."

JESUS WARNED, BE READY
THE BIBLICAL MODEL OF SUDDEN DISASTERS

GOD DOES THINGS SUDDENLY

One of the principles in the Bible is that things happen suddenly. In God's kingdom, anything with lasting impact happens suddenly.

1. God created the universe and world suddenly.
2. God created Eve suddenly.
3. Sin entered the world suddenly.
4. Noah's flood came suddenly.
5. God came to Abraham suddenly.
6. God came to Moses suddenly.
7. God brought His people out of Egypt suddenly.
8. God raised up Joseph to be second in command to Pharaoh suddenly.
9. Jesus came as a baby suddenly.
10. Jesus was crucified suddenly.

> Have no fear of **sudden** disaster
> or of the ruin that overtakes the wicked,
> (Proverbs 3:25).

> **Suddenly** the fingers of a human hand appeared and wrote on the plaster of the wall, near the lampstand in the royal palace. The king watched the hand as it wrote. His face turned pale and he was so frightened that his knees knocked together and his legs gave way (Daniel 5:5-6).

> **Suddenly** a great company of the heavenly host appeared with the angel, praising God and saying,

"Glory to God in the highest, and on earth peace to men on whom his favor rests" (Luke 2:13-14).

Suddenly a sound like the blowing of a violent wind came from heaven and filled the whole house where they were sitting. They saw what seemed to be tongues of fire that separated and came to rest on each of them (Acts 2:2-3).

Suddenly an angel of the Lord appeared and a light shone in the cell. He struck Peter on the side and woke him up. "Quick, get up!" he said, and the chains fell off Peter's wrists (Acts 12:7).

Now, brothers, about times and dates we do not need to write to you, for you know very well that the day of the Lord will come like a thief in the night. While people are saying, "Peace and safety," destruction will come on them suddenly, as labor pains on a pregnant woman, and they will not escape (1 Thessalonians 5:1-3).

As it relates to an economic disaster, God, who is continually causing all things to work together for the worlds' good, will surely cause things to **suddenly** "go berserk."

A BIBLICAL EXAMINATION: IS GOD INVOLVED IN ECONOMIC DISASTERS?

Could God be involved in an economic disaster, the last days notwithstanding? Let us look at the Bible to find situations where God used economic disaster to warn people.

First, during the days of Moses, Egypt experienced an economic disaster when God brought the Jews out of Egypt. The Egyptians lost all of their means of production.

Second, God brought seven years of famine to Egypt during Joseph's time after seven good years.

> "Then bring your livestock," said Joseph. "I will sell you food in exchange for your livestock, since your money is gone." So they brought their livestock to Joseph, and he gave them food in exchange for their horses, their sheep and goats, their cattle and donkeys. And he brought them through that year with food in exchange for all their livestock (Genesis 47:16-17).

Joseph exchanged food for what we would now consider production equipment: horses like our modern cars, sheep and goats like our equipment for making clothing or milk and cheese, cattle like our tractors, and donkeys like our trucks. The Egyptians eventually sold housing material and their land, which is the basis for the production of all products.

A third example can be found in the book of Judges. When the people were blessed, they eventually turned away from God. God brought disaster on them, so they cried out and God delivered them. The cycle repeated. The equivalent today would be that God orchestrates economic cycles, including long stock market cycles. When God blesses, people indulge in pleasure, and then God brings correction patterns and cycles through market corrections. If government tries to negate these corrections, the eventual market correction is even greater, since government is fighting against God's correction. This cycle is the pattern we see in the book of Judges.

A fourth example is described in Revelation 18:15-18.

> "The merchants who sold these things and gained their wealth from her will stand far off, terrified at her torment. They will weep and mourn and cry out:
> "'Woe! Woe, O great city,
> dressed in fine linen, purple and scarlet,

and glittering with gold, precious stones and pearls!
In one hour such great wealth has been brought to ruin!'
"Every sea captain, and all who travel by ship, the sailors, and all who earn their living from the sea, will stand
far off. When they see the smoke of her burning, they
will exclaim, 'Was there ever a city like this great city?'"

These are just a few examples, but the Bible is full of examples
of God warning His people or the Gentile nations around them. His
discipline was economic disaster affecting the food supply, food production, housing, or the distribution of food and goods. God knows
people pay attention when their pockets have holes.

GOD HAS A REASON FOR MOVING SUDDENLY

We do not respond in the manner that God desires, except when
God moves suddenly. God desires we respond to His discipline. If
God moved slowly, we would adapt like a frog in water. We would not
respobd if God took 30 years to bring discipline.

WHAT DID JESUS SAY ABOUT MOVING SUDDENLY?

Starting with Jesus is always a good idea.

"Who then is the faithful and wise servant, whom the
master has put in charge of the servants in his house-
hold to give them their food at the proper time? It will
be good for that servant whose master finds him doing
so when he returns. I tell you the truth, he will put him
in charge of all his possessions. But suppose that servant is wicked and says to himself, 'My master is staying away a long time,' and he then begins to beat his
fellow servants and to eat and drink with drunkards.
The master of that servant will come on a day when he

does not expect him and at an hour he is not aware of"
(Matthew 24: 45-50, emphasis my own).

Teachers love these kinds of passages, especially the parables. They can go off in many different directions. They can stay close to Jesus' meaning, or they can freely wander a little. The important thing is to stay close to the main teaching and not go off on rabbit trails to use the parable to confirm personal agenda. I will try to stay off rabbit trails.

Jesus' main practical focus is the "faithful and wise servant," who has been put in charge of whatever Jesus has given him. In essence, Jesus has given us the whole world and all of our resources, including ourselves. The faithful and wise servant keeps doing what God has called him to do twenty-four hours a day, seven days a week, to serve others, and he continues to do so because "the master of that servant will come on a day when he does not expect him." Included in this parable is the detail that the master will return suddenly when the servant does not expect.

I believe that God uses economic disasters to bring warning and discipline on all nations, including His believers. The economic disaster will fall on all, but the believers should be ready. "He causes his sun to rise on the evil and the good, and sends rain on the righteous and the unrighteous" (Matthew 5:45). Are you ready?

GOD IS INVOLVED IN ECONOMIC DISASTERS

Taleb, Buchanan, and Minsky all recognized that Black Swans, upheavals, sudden and tumultuous changes, cataclysmic and ubiquitous events, or Minsky Moments are unpredictable and happen quite regularly throughout history at unpredictable intervals, triggered by seemingly small events.

Taleb and Buchanan focus their main events on world structures and science, and Taleb and Minsky focus on economic and financial events when things are likely to break down.

Taking from these three secular authors, I willl take the liberty of making a Biblical statement. God is ubiquitous, and He is working in and through all things. What God does affects all things. We cannot fully predict what God will do, but because we have His Word, we can understand a little about how God works. We understand that His hand is orchestrating good for the world and for His children who trust Him. I believe that God is somehow involved in all Black Swans, ubiquitous calamities, and Minsky Moments.

God wants His believers to sing what Matt Redman wrote in his song "Blessed be Your Name."[18]

> Every blessing You pour out
> I'll turn back to praise.
> When the darkness closes in, Lord,
> Still I will say.
>
> Blessed be the name of the Lord
> Blessed be Your name.
> Blessed be the name of the Lord
> Blessed be Your glorious name.
>
> You give and take away
> You give and take away.
> My heart will choose to say,
> Lord, blessed be Your name.

ECONOMIC DISASTER COULD TRIGGER FOOD SHORTAGES AND FAMINE DUE TO THE DEMISE OF THE DOLLAR

If we could show a simple graph of current economic trends, we would see economic prosperity would be headed down. An earlier chart shows the declining value of the dollar over the past fifty years. The danger is if the dollar were to fall and if its fall resembled a parabolic crash. If this were to happen, not only would the economic conditions, financial conditions, and governmental support for social services seriously deteriorate, the structural support systems for equitable food distribution would break down worldwide, which would impact people's food supply.

Presently, the main group of people who do not have sufficient food, either due to a breakdown in food distribution due to inefficiencies or government corruption, are people in Third World countries. If an economic disaster of titanic proportions were to occur, the food shortage would very quickly affect millions of people in the middle class. Many would lose their jobs and lack sufficient food, possibly due to the following conditions.

1. Trucking or shipping and transportation companies have trouble operating due to strikes for higher wages or benefits as companies try to cut wages and benefits in order to survive.

2. A shortage of fuel occurs or the cost of fuel dramatically increases (imagine oil at $200 per gallon) due to a collapse of the US dollar, the US dollar no longer holding its reserve status, a crisis in the Middle East if Iran closed the Straits of Hormuz, or a war in the Middle East if someone attacked Israel and they struck back.

These scenarios are eerie and seem like scenes that could only happen in a movie, but we are not far from a small, local event triggering and creating a disastrous scenario. If this were to happen, there would be rioting in the streets which could snowball into a long-term disaster. At this point, there are already signs of dissatisfaction as people rioted in many Muslim countries, resulting in the overthrow of leaders who previously seemed to be firmly in control of their nations. There are many different groups of unsatisfied people, but one common thread among them is their desire for economic fairness for all. In Greece, Spain, and France, people rioted as they refused to submit to governments that were trying to be fiscally responsible. If those in Germany join in, although for the different reason of being tired of fixing Europe's problems, the rest of Europe could be in for a long winter. All of these potential scenarios come down to economics and could very quickly flare up if food were to become too expensive or scarce.

Could you and your family thrive in this environment? Is Jesus enough?

ARE WE MISSING SOMETHING?

George Santayana wrote, "Those who cannot remember the past are condemned to repeat it" (*The Life of Reason*). The Bible writes it this way.

> For I do not want you to be ignorant of the fact, brothers, that our forefathers were all under the cloud and that they all passed through the sea. They were all baptized into Moses in the cloud and in the sea. They all ate the same spiritual food and drank the same spiritual drink; for they drank from the spiritual rock that accompanied them, and that rock was Christ. Nevertheless, God was not pleased with most of them; their bodies were scattered over the desert. Now these things occurred as examples to keep us from setting our hearts on evil things as they did (1 Corinthians 10:1-6).

> The Israelites did evil in the eyes of the Lord; they forgot the Lord their God and served the Baals and the Asherahs. The anger of the Lord burned against Israel so that he sold them into the hands of Cushan-Rishathaim king of Aram Naharaim, to whom the Israelites were subject for eight years. But when they cried out to the Lord, he raised up for them a deliverer, Othniel son of Kenaz, Caleb's younger brother, who saved them (Judges 3:7-10).

From these verses, we see clearly God's heart. God blessed His chosen nation Israel, but they needed to stay connected to Him. When they did not, the result was that "their bodies were scattered over the desert." When they did "evil in the eyes of the Lord" and "forgot the Lord their God… the anger of the Lord burned against Israel…" God warned His people over and over through the prophets to turn back to Him. When they did not, God removed His hedge of protection, and He brought the Assyrian, Babylonians, the Medo-Persians, the Greeks, and the Romans against them.

God has blessed America abundantly in its first two hundred years of existence. The blessings came because the founding fathers recognized God and set up laws that came from God's laws. America's laws were not laws enforced by power, guns, or threats, but they were moral and just laws that believed in giving freedom to all who lived in America. They were not perfect laws, e.g. slavery, but like God's laws, they enabled Americans to move towards a better life with God as the foundation. The following are some examples of how America's foundation was rooted in God.

1. AMERICA NO LONGER FOLLOWS THE DECLARATION OF INDEPENDENCE.

> When in the Course of human events, it becomes necessary for one people to dissolve the political bands which have connected them with another, and to assume among the powers of the earth, the separate and equal station to which the Laws of Nature and of Nature's God entitle them, a decent respect to the opinions of mankind requires that they should declare the causes which impel them to the separation.

> We hold these truths to be self-evident, that all men are created equal, that they are endowed by their **Creator**

with certain unalienable Rights, that among these are
Life, Liberty and the pursuit of Happiness.

We in America have forgotten the centricity of God in our country. We have allowed small groups of people to change the laws of the
land, and as a result, America has taken God out of many of the
important areas of life that made America great. Our businesses do
not operate with God in mind. Our educational system has removed
God from our schools. God cannot be found in our government or
political system. Forty to fifty million babies have been aborted over
the past fifty years.

God looks down at America, and what does He see? First, He
sees many praying people, and He is pleased with them. What else
does He see, and how did we get here? God is distressed with much of
what He sees. America has abandoned God.

2. BUSINESS AND POLITICS ARE RULED BY PSYCHOPATHS (EXCEPT FOR YOU).

Businesses used to be controlled by men of moral character, and
they used wisdom and concern for others as guiding factors in running their businesses. The pace of business was slow and change was
slow. That is no longer the case. The pace of information and change
has been increasing exponentially.

Ray Pensador writes that the business and political worlds are
ruled by psychopaths. He defines how normal people react. "By 'normal,' what I mean is that people tend to say and do things in accordance to their real thoughts, emotions, views, ideas, beliefs. In other
words, in a 'what-you-see-is-what-you-get' mode."[19] He then defines
the psychopath. "By contrast, the high-functioning psychopath is
"characterized primarily by a lack of empathy and remorse, shallow
emotions, egocentricity, and deceptiveness."[20] Because of their char-
acteristics, they tend to rule the world. They rise to the highest levels of power in politics and business. Pensador continues, "If you are

ambitious and choose to get involved in power-plays, the first thing you need to recognize is that you have to leave your values, emotions, ideals, and most high-minded human traits, 'at the door' (as it were), if you want to have a shot to become the 'top dog.'"[21]

In the past, these psycopaths would have been pigeon-holed in business. Very few would have been trusted, and therefore, they would not have been able to reach the top of corporate America. Many early corporate leaders, especially owners of companies who cared about people, recognized that the new breed of psychopaths that rule today would not make satisfactory managers of people. Today that is no longer the case. Profit rules, and how businesses get it does not matter. How profit is gained does matter to those who pray.

3. GOD IS MISSING FROM THE EDUCATIONAL SYSTEM.

No one would argue the point that God has been completely removed from the educational system. I will not argue about original intent. It is plain for all to see that God is not there. Since 1962, when prayer (Engel v. Vitale) was removed from schools, and since 1963, when Bible reading (Abington School District v. Schempp) was removed, small groups of people have systematically and effectively removed God from the school system. The Ten Commandments cannot be displayed, lest we corrupt our youth by forbidding them to kill.

While I agree that it is not be right to brainwash children towards any religion, a small group of people have seen to it that it is not possible to teach character and values in schools today.

In the late 1980s, I was invited to a teacher's seminar with close to two hundred teachers and educators present. The head of the local electrical union and I were invited along with a few others. As I recall, the group was interested in hearing from business people concerning what they could focus on regarding how to educate students for careers in business. My kids were involved heavily in judo, and I shared an episode from one of the judo matches. One of the youths from our club had lost a match and threw a mini tantrum at the referee. He thought the call was unfair. I concluded that I thought the educational system needed to focus more on honor, integrity, humility, and respect. All of the others speakers received polite applause from the audience, while I was met with complete silence. I was not yet a believer so I did not understand what was happening. The group thought I was pushing my Christian beliefs into the educational system. Of course Diana had a more practical view: "You were junk!"

Lessons from Governor Mike Huckabee

Former Arkansas Governor Mike Huckabee commented on the December 2012 Sandy Hook Elementary School shooting. "We ask why there's violence in our schools, but we've systematically removed God from our schools. Should we be so surprised that schools become a place of carnage, because we've made it a place where we don't want to talk about eternity, life, what responsibility means, accountability. That we're not just going to have to be accountable to the police if they catch us, but one day we stand before a holy God and judgment. If we don't believe that, then we don't fear that. And so, I sometimes when people say, 'Why did God let it happen?' you know, God wasn't armed, he didn't go to the school. God will be there in the form of a lot of people with hugs and with therapy and in a whole lot of ways in which I think he will be involved in the aftermath. Maybe we ought to let him in on the front end, and we wouldn't have to call him when it's all said and done on the back end."[22]

I touch upon these areas to make an important point. There seems to be a huge disconnect between the America in which we live today and the America of the first half of the twentieth century. It seems that something happened to America after World War II. Did we get proud and arrogant as a nation because we helped the world against Germany, Italy, and Japan in their quest for world domination? Did we think to ourselves, "We are the greatest nation on earth ever?" Did we forget from where we came? Did we forget what made America great? Did we forget our God? Granted, not everyone loved God before 1950, but we had a critical mass of believers. We trusted God in our monetary and political systems, we trusted God in our schools, and we trusted God in the wombs of women.

4. IS ABORTION RIGHT IN GOD'S EYES?

Small groups of people have effectively changed the laws of America so that aborting babies is legal. It really does not matter if the laws of all the countries in the world say that it is legal to abort a baby because God does not see it that way. These groups continually move the line of the law to redefine when a baby is fully human. I will not get into the discussion of righteous abortions or the safety of the mother's life. My focus here is to bring attention to the many babies that have been aborted in America and around the world.

As I look at the world and America today through God's eyes, I think God must really be upset. He is upset not just with the few that have removed God from their businesses, those responsible for our political and educational systems, or those participating in the abortions, but He is upset with believers as well, myself included. We do not stand up for righteousness reigning in these areas as we go about our religious duties and practices. We pray for ourselves, our families, our businesses, even our government and leaders. However, God's view of prayer and fasting is a little different. Something is missing.

5. SINGLES RULE. THE BIGGEST DISEASE IS "ME-ITIS."

Gary Halbert, an investment guru, wrote an article about the US birth rate, asking, "How did we become a nation of singles?" Halbert analyzed the singles trend in demographics, drew a correlation with the US birth rate, and commented on the impact that singles had on the recent presidential election and will have on the future of the United States. He cited some interesting statistics.

- People who are "ever-married," marry at some point in their lives. Between 1910 and 1970, this percentage of the population varied between 92.8% and 98.3%. Since 1970, this group has declined so that by 2000, it stood at 88.6%.

- According to the 2010 Census, almost 24% of men and 19% of women between 35 and 44 years of age, have never been married. Of people between 20 and 34 years of age, the prime childbearing years, 67% of men and 57% of women have never been married. Over half of the voting-age population is single. About 10-15% of the population do not get married for the first time until they near retirement.

- Geographically, singles tend to live in cities. As urban density increases, marriage rates (and childbearing rates) decrease.

- Multiple studies quantitate the US fertility rate among women as 1.9 children and falling. Any fertility rate below 2.1 children per woman will result in a declining population.

- Halbert cites Jonathan Last, who did research and wrote an article for the *Weekly Standard*.

  "The second shift is the dismantling of the iron triangle of sex, marriage, and childbearing. Beginning in roughly 1970, the mastery of contraception decoupled sex from babymaking. And with that link broken, the connections between sex and marriage—and finally between marriage and childrearing—were severed, too."[23]

Jonathan's Last's conclusion is a sad commentary on America. It is evident that people meet, partner together for a season, live together for a year or two, and then move on. Sociologists, politicians, government leaders, believers, and even Christian leaders, are saying that people are going to live this way and that it is impossible to try to change the way it is. What is God's view?

> God blessed them and said to them, "Be fruitful and **increase in number**; fill the earth and subdue it..." (Genesis 1:28, NIV, emphasis my own).

From the beginning, God's instruction to Adam and all mankind was to increase in number. God created the family model with which to do this. God loves babies, fathers, and mothers. The family is the hundredfold blessing. God's heart always wanted the family to be the foundation of His blessings for us.

America and a large portion of the developed nations have turned away completely from God's model. Of the twenty countries with the highest Gross Domestic Product, only India (2.58), Mexico (2.27), Indonesia (2.23), and Turkey (2.13) have fertility rates that will cause their countries to increase in number. The magic number is 2.1 for a stable population. The rest of the countries are declining, some slow, some very fast. Japan (1.39), Greece (1.39), Italy (1.4), and Germany (1.41) bring up the bottom of fertility rates, while France is at 2.08.[24]

I wonder if God is saddened by what is happening in America as well as the developed nations of the world, which are the nations He has blessed. People turn away from God and turn away from His ways and His instructions "to increase." People enjoy sex without the responsibilities of raising a family. While all sin is bad, maybe this displeases God the most, as it affects the family and the part of the family that He loves the most: babies.

GOD IS WARNING US THAT WE ARE WAY OFF TRACK

RIVERS AND DROUGHTS

George Friedman, one of the geopolitical experts in the world today, writes that America has "some of the richest agricultural land in the world. Even more important, it is a land with a superb system of navigable rivers that allowed the country's agricultural surplus to be shipped to world markets, creating a class of businessmen-farmers that is unique in history."[26]

Friedman writes in his book that no other nation in the world has a combination of rich agricultural land and river systems, as well as outlets to the sea, like America has. None of that is of any value without rain. Could God be withholding rain from America today to warn us?

As I write this (December 2012), the Mississippi River is fifteen to twenty feet below normal to a fifty-year low. Its nominal depth is thirteen feet. Experts say if the depth drops to nine feet or lower, all barge traffic will be severely affected, and most will stop completely. This would cause an economic disaster if the depth stayed below nine feet for an extended period of time. What is the cause of the low water levels? The cause is drought conditions. America is having its worst drought this year (2012) since 1934.

The Great Depression was after the Roaring Twenties. Is it possible that God was warning America while they were living it up from 1920 to 1929 and in the following years? It was as if He might have been upset. He blessed America with so much, but "people were eating and drinking, marrying and giving in marriage," mostly concerned with making money and taking care of themselves, like people in Noah's day. "For in the days before the flood, people were eating and drinking, marrying and giving in marriage, up to the day Noah entered the ark; and they knew nothing about what would happen

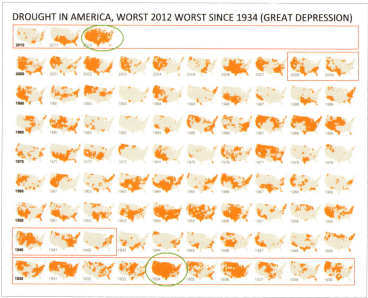

DROUGHT IN AMERICA, WORST 2012 WORST SINCE 1934 (GREAT DEPRESSION)

National Climatic Data Center, National Oceanic and Atmospheric Administration

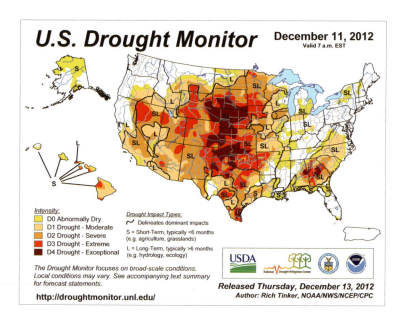

until the flood came and took them all away. That is how it will be at the coming of the Son of Man" (Matthew 24:38-39).

If God brought the flood during Noah's time and again caused droughts in 1931, 1934, and 1936, after the economic depression that took place from 1929 to 1932, America might be wise to wake up to the signs of the times. We would not expect the secular world to believe this, but believers who have God's Word as their guide should pay attention. Was the Depression a time when America could have returned to God and possibly did not? God brought a drought and continued withholding rain.

We have always had natural calamities, but they seem to be hitting us harder the past few years. Earthquakes, tsunamis, tornadoes, and hurricanes are taking place with increasing frequency and intensity. Could God be warning America that it is on the wrong path? Could God be warning America through the wars around the world by instigating other countries against America? If so, God is operating in a different realm from the one we see. Here are a few instances of God moving through the spirit realm.

GOD'S WARNINGS COME THROUGH THE SPIRITUAL REALM

"Satan rose up against Israel and incited David to take a census of Israel" (1 Chronicles 21:1). "Again the anger of the Lord burned against Israel, and he incited David against them, saying, 'Go and take a census of Israel and Judah'" (2 Samuel 24:1). Notice that God was warning Israel to get back on track so He used Satan to incite David to take a census to count the number of fighting men, and He disciplined Israel.

In 2 Chronicles 18, Ahab tried to convince Jehoshaphat to go to war with him against Ramoth Gilead. Four hundred prophets told Ahab and Jehoshaphat to go and that they would have victory. Jehoshaphat requested one honest prophet. They called Micaiah, and after a little dance, he told them the truth.

> Micaiah continued, "Therefore hear the word of the Lord: I saw the Lord sitting on his throne with all the host of heaven standing on his right and on his left. And the Lord said, **'Who will entice Ahab king of Israel into attacking Ramoth Gilead and going to his death there?'**
> "One suggested this, and another that. Finally, a spirit came forward, stood before the Lord and said, 'I will entice him.'
> "'By what means?' the Lord asked.
> "'I will go and be a lying spirit in the mouths of all his prophets,' he said.
> "'You will succeed in enticing him,' said the Lord. 'Go and do it.'
> "So now the Lord has put a lying spirit in the mouths of these prophets of yours. The Lord has decreed disaster for you" (2 Chronicles 18:18-22, emphasis my own).

God effectively used this means to bring Ahab to his death.

I believe if God does not use some form of discipline to warn America, He will have to apologize to Ahab, Israel, Sodom and Gomorrah, Egypt, the people during Noah's days, and a host of other nations that experienced his discipline. I will not use the term "judgment," but I think it is a "warning" to get America back on track. Final judgment is reserved for the end. This means that some of what is happening now is God's discipline. This is good since God is causing all things to work together for the good of America.

THE TOWER OF BABEL REVISITED

We should be able to tell what things displease God, resulting in His warnings. One thing that displeased God was the Tower of Babel. People became proud and arrogant and wanted to become great, and in essence, they rebelled against God so He gave them different languages to keep them separate. "Come, let us go down and confuse their language so they will not understand each other" (Genesis 11:7).

J. Vernon McGee's commentary says, "Down through the centuries mankind has been kept separate, and it has been a great hindrance to him. One thing that is happening today through the medium of radio and television and jet travel is that these walls are bring broken down. This is one reason that I believe God is coming down in **judgment** again."[27]

McGee wrote his commentary in 1981, and much more has changed in the world as far as the walls being broken down. Computers, along with the internet, cell phones, smart phones, and social media, such as Facebook, have exponentially increased the connectivity of the different races, and we effectively have a flat world today. We are moving towards a one-world government through the United Nations and already essentially have a one-world financial and economic system. The world's powers in control "play ball" together, and it is beginning to look a lot like "Booth Park Rules."

I would not use the term judgment as McGee has done here, because it communicates something different in the secular world and in the minds of those who may use the term today. Most now think of God's final judgment so I will use the idea that God is now disciplining us by warning us of impending judgment to come and wants to warn believers and non-believers alike to turn from their wicked ways. Even believers, myself included, are living in ways that do not please God. I think the things God is displeased with today will shock most of us when we see Him face to face.

GOD IS WORKING FOR OUR GOOD BY WARNING US

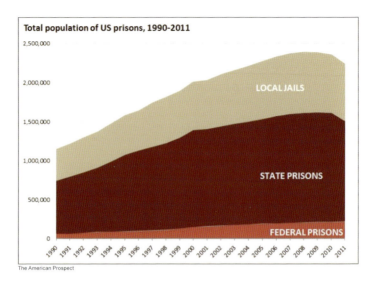

The American Prospect

All types of crime statistics are off the charts. Could this be a symptom of the most deadly disease of all time: "Me-itis?" You could look up other statistics on the ills of our nation. However, you really do not need to look at statistics because you can see wickedness all around you, on television, in movies, in magazines, and in newspapers. Violence, crime, evil, and greed are suffocating America. By one calculation, there were eighteen mass shootings in the year 2012 alone.

I believe that God has been warning America for the past thirty or forty years. The good news is our God is patient and "not wanting anyone to perish" (2 Peter 3:9), but how long can this go on before God brings down His upraised hand (Isaiah 9:12, 17) upon America and the world? I think His discipline will come soon, not because I want disaster to happen, but because I know God's nature and what He has written. The passages in 1 Corinthians 10 and Judges 3 listed previously are just a few of many where God warns us by using Israel as His example. He wants us to restore our broken relationship with

Him. Surely, America has believers who will recognize the signs and be the first to carry His banner and wave it high above the nations of the earth. 2 Chronicles 7:14 says, "If my people, who are called by my name, will humble themselves and pray and seek my face and turn from their wicked ways, then I will hear from heaven, and I will forgive their sin and will heal their land" repentance starts with believers.

THE WAY BACK

The Bible gives us a glimpse of God's heart, and we can still learn from His heart today. Small groups of people in America have lived any way they wanted and contrary to God's ways. They have changed laws and usurped power in the political, financial, business, educational, and moral worlds. They have influenced the public in general. These groups may have learned from Hitler who shrewdly analyzed people.

"What luck for rulers that men do not think."

"Those who want to live, let them fight, and those who do not want to fight in this world of eternal struggle do not deserve to live."

"The man who has no sense of history, is like a man who has no ears or eyes"

"The receptivity of the masses is very limited, their intelligence is small, but their power of forgetting is enormous. In consequence of these facts, all effective propaganda must be limited to a very few points and must harp on these in slogans until the last member of the public understands what you want him to understand by your slogan."

Even some believers have much explaining to do when
    they meet God, who spoke to us through Isaiah.
'Why have we fasted,' they say,
    'and you have not seen it?
Why have we humbled ourselves,
    and you have not noticed?'

"Yet on the day of your fasting, you do as you please
    and exploit all your workers.
Is this the kind of fast I have chosen,
    only a day for man to humble himself?
Is it only for bowing one's head like a reed
    and for lying in sackcloth and ashes?
Is that what you call a fast,
    a day acceptable to the Lord?
"Is not this the kind of fasting I have chosen:
to loose the chains of injustice
    and untie the cords of the yoke,
to set the oppressed free
    and break every yoke?
Is it not to share your food with the hungry
    and to provide the poor wanderer with shelter—
when you see the naked, to clothe him,
    and not to turn away from your own flesh and blood?
Then your light will break forth like the dawn,
    and your healing will quickly appear;
then your righteousness will go before you,
    and the glory of the Lord will be your rear guard.
Then you will call, and the Lord will answer;
    you will cry for help, and he will say: Here am I
    (Isaiah 58:3, 5-9)

I will be the first to admit I am not even close to pleasing God completely in the things that break His heart listed in this passage in Isaiah. I rejoice that God in His grace and mercy towards America is giving us ample opportunity to make things right with Him. I believe it must start with believers. We must be prepared so we can help others in need when the time comes. The warnings from God will grow in frequency and intensity, and wars, droughts, famines, earthquakes, tsunamis, and storms will increase. We should remember that throughout the Bible God used these same calamities to warn His people Israel to turn back to Him and follow His ways.

In our preparation, we cannot go into our holes or caves and hide until the upraised hand of the Lord strikes. We need to join together in unity (John 17) and reach out through all means. The body of Christ must be one so that the world recognizes God is with us.

BE READY BY HOLDING THE ULITMATE MONEY: GOLD

MONEY AND THE GOLD STANDARD

Ever since I can remember, I have had a love for money. I do not know when or how that happened. Maybe it happened when I was about six or seven years old, when I looked in one of my dad's drawers and found a whole stack of unused checks. I thought we were rich. No one explained to me that you needed money to write those checks. One day I found my dad's coin box where he kept all his loose change, mostly pennies, nickels, dimes, and some quarters. This confirmed it for me: we were rich. I could not understand why they gave me only a quarter and a nickel for lunch. Can you believe lunch was twenty-five cents, and an extra box of milk was a nickel? That was what we received for our allowance each day, even into intermediate school.

At Kawananakoa Intermediate School, I remember a friend told me he received five dollars per week for his allowance. I was sure his dad was a millionaire and had only quarters and dollar bills in his coin box. Some of my friends would go down the street to a small store where they would buy a small bowl of fried rice for ten cents. I envied them. I could not afford that, and there was no way I was going to ask my mom for money to buy something so unnecessary.

During my childhood, the Nuuanu YMCA was located at the corner of Vineyard Boulevard and Pali Highway in Honolulu. They had just started to build the H-1 Freeway. The best bargain at the "Y" was the gravy and rice for ten cents. When I mashed up the gravy and rice, there was so much gravy, and it was so delicious. You could order two scoops of rice for fifteen cents, but they still gave you the same amount of gravy, just one ladleful, which made the rice a little dry. I struggled with the decision. Should I buy one scoop of rice with "choke" gravy or two scoops with just enough gravy? Should I choose quantity or quality in the age-old quandary? It was at these times that I wished I had more money so I would not have to make that choice. I envied those who could have the gravy, rice, and a small hamburger. The YMCA made the best burgers. During my first summer spent at the YMCA, I had a cheeseburger and macaroni salad every single day. If I told mom what I was ordering, she gave me enough money to cover the costs, but nothing extra. My mom was wise. Maybe people who grow up during hard times become wise.

The Bible says, "the love of money is a root of all kinds of evil" (1 Timothy 6:10). Even if I had known that in my preteen and teen years, I am sure it would not have made a bit of a difference. In my formative years, I could see what went on in the world around me. I may not have loved money, but I sure loved the things it could buy and the freedom that came with having money.I resolved in my heart that I wanted to do well when I grew up.

I have since changed my view of money and have tried to align myself with God's thoughts on money. As I write this, keep in mind that these are my opinions and thoughts and are not meant to be investment advice.

Here is my opinion on money today: gold is the ultimate money. I believe gold is money because God made it to be used as money. I will not spend time trying to convince you of this truth. I feel this explanation is important because of what is happening in the world today, which may affect everyone. The powers in control are printing money, and the value of paper money is depreciating at a dangerous rate. This is happening in almost all nations and could end up as the crisis that tips the scales into the greatest economic disaster ever. I am not predicting such a disaster, but I believe that unless the policies of the powers in control change so that the economy is under control, the probability of a disaster continues to increase.

A SIMPLIFIED VIEW OF GOLD

When gold is mentioned, people may think about instant riches. The Gold Rush, Fort Knox, and the James Bond movie *Goldfinger* are some of the things that might come to mind when gold is mentioned. Gold has an allure, some of which is due to the thought of riches and some of which is due to Hollywood hype because we have all

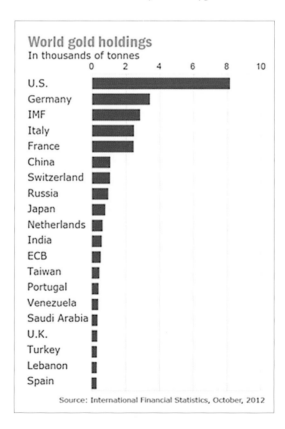

World gold holdings
In thousands of tonnes

Source: International Financial Statistics, October, 2012

seen pictures of gold stored underground in the mystical Fort Knox glamorized by James Bond. We know gold has value and is currently in the range of $1,700 per ounce. Ten years ago it was valued around $300 per ounce. We may think that if we had only bought some gold then, we would be rich.

I touch upon gold because the powers in control, as well as the media, have caused much confusion concerning gold's relationship to money. They make fun of gold bugs and treat them as gold nuts. They know gold is ultimately tied to money. Look at who owns most of the gold in the world.

THE HISTORY OF GOLD

Prior to 700 BC, most trade took place under a barter system, and if gold or silver was used as a means of exchange, the measurement was based on the weight of gold or silver. The earliest references to gold or silver refer to either pieces of golf or silver or in some versions of the Bible, the weight of gold or silver measured as a shekel. Transactions in the Bible were based purely on weight.

Around 700 BC, gold coins were "invented" and were "designed to get around the tedious business of weighting and checking purity… The Egyptians were casting gold bars as money as early as 4000BC, each bar stamped with the name of the pharaoh Menes" (Peter Bernstein, *The Power of Gold*, pages 24-25).

Joseph was sold to the Ishmaelites traders for twenty shekels of silver (NIV) or twenty pieces of silver (NKJV, NLT). All through the Bible, gold and silver were used for buying and selling, essentially, as money for value transactions.

In 1787, Ephraim Brasher, a goldsmith in New York, minted the oldest American gold coin. It contained 26.4 grams of 22-carat gold. The first US gold coin was the $10 gold piece, or Eagle, minted in 1795. The first design featured a bust of Liberty and an eagle with a wreath above its head on the reverse side.

I believe God made gold to be used as money, and in His infinite wisdom, He knew that gold, as with money, gave the world a balancing mechanism which helped prevent runaway spending by the powers in control. Let me use two countries, France and England, for explanation purposes. Let us think back to the year 1900. Merchants from France and England would buy goods from each other. If a French merchant had really good products, say Gucci bags, the English would buy them. If Englishmen were to buy thousands of Gucci bags, the French would end up with lots of English pound sterlings. The French merchant could turn the money into the French government, and the French government could exchange the pounds for gold at the day's current rate. The French government could then go to England and exchange the pounds for gold, thereby reducing the gold England had in reserve.

The result would be that gold would move from England to France. France would be richer in gold, and England would be richer in Gucci bags. Eventually the French wealth would increase, and they would start buying English goods. The process would reverse, and gold would flow back to England.

Gold was a means of keeping crazy consumer spending in check or in balance. It also kept the governments in check since they could not expand their currency beyond their wealth in gold.

THE BRETTON WOODS SYSTEM IMPLEMENTATION AND FAILURE

Near the end of World War II, the powers in control needed a mechanism to facilitate rebuilding efforts after the war ended. The Bretton Woods system was devised. The main element of the system was that each country was required to adopt a "monetary policy that maintained the exchange rate by tying its currency to the US dollar and the ability of the International Monetary Fund (IMF) to bridge temporary imbalances of payments."[26] Any country could exchange their US dollars for American gold as they desired. "On August 15, 1971, the United States unilaterally terminated convertibility of the US dollar to gold... At the same time, many fixed currencies became free floating."[28]

Since 1971, we have a hodgepodge of currency solutions, which has allowed much more freedom for the powers in control to increase their money supply. The old checks and balances are gone, and in times of emergencies, the floodgates seem to open to solve the financial credit problems that countries have. No doubt, these are real problems, and no one truly knows the solutions to the myriad of monetary, fiscal, credit, debt, unemployment, and social and welfare issues that curse countries today.

One thing seems certain. Each country is forced to exponentially increase their money as well as their credit supply in order to stave off political, social, banking, recession, and depression fears that exists within their borders.

SO WHAT?

The governments of the world are holding gold to back their currencies, but they will not exchange their currencies for the ultimate money, gold. Why not? Could it be that they make fun of gold on the surface, but know that gold is the ultimate store of value, which we call money? Allow me to describe a Hawaiian example. If you went to Las Vegas and bought chips, gambled for one week and then went to cash in your chips, how would you feel if the hotel told you that they would not exchange them?

Why are they holding all that gold and telling the public that gold is an ancient relic? Do they not believe it is the ultimate monetary hedge?

God speaks through the Bible, and the Bible seems to treat gold as money, a medium of exchange and a store of value. If there was a sudden monetary collapse in which our US dollar (paper currency) was losing value quickly, what would you do to protect yourself? The thing to do would be to pray, pray, and pray.

Unfortunately, if you wait for the dollar to collapse, there will be little you could do in reaction to a fast falling dollar. If you are wealthy and have a net worth of millions of dollars, you may not need to do anything as you may be alright financially. If you have a million-dollar spiritual life also, you are in splendid shape. If not, read on.

BE READY: COPY JOSEPH

I remember what Pastor Allen Cardines of Hope Chapel Nanakuli taught us about civil defense. You cannot take care of others in an emergency if you cannot take care yourself. The best way to prepare for a natural disaster is to have your food and emergency supplies ready, and then you might be ready to help others.

If the worst happens, and there are many scenarios that could cause an economic disaster, could you survive? We like to think Jesus is enough, but could you survive a ten-percent reduction in your income level and standard of living? What about a thirty-percent reduction? What about a fifty-percent reduction? You say that is impossible, but God says nothing is impossible. A family living off of $100,000 of income each year would reduce their level of consumption and expenses to $90,000, $70,000, or at the 50% reduction, to $50,000. Is that possible?

You might say, if I had to, I could. I am not here to tell you what you can and cannot do, but as I look at the possibilities, within the next three to five years, or even five to ten years, there is a very high likelihood of an economic disaster unfolding in some form or another.

Is it possible to have a stock or bond market crash, which could affect your job or your retirement savings? Maybe a dollar crash would make things you bought twice as expensive, like gas, eggs, bread, and meats. What if gas were $8 per gallon and bread were $5 a loaf?

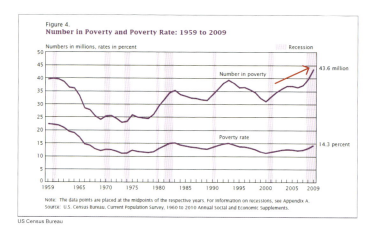

Figure 4.
Number in Poverty and Poverty Rate: 1959 to 2009

US Census Bureau

Would Jesus still be enough? Would you be able to thrive?

What if you had time to adjust, say the next two years? Would you be able to slowly reduce consumption, pay off debts, rearrange your priorities, realign your expectations, readjust your thinking towards the minimum income, and increase your savings? What type of vacation would you take? How would you plan for education or retirement? Would those two years make a difference?

What if your family realigned its priorities, made cutbacks, adjusted expectations, and lived together in one bigger expanded house instead of two or three separate houses? Would those changes help you thrive? What if you realigned your priorities to line up with Jesus' priorities, and you found that life was even better?

These are just some things to think about to help you thrive.

Genesis 37-50 provides us a model through the story of Joseph. In summary, when Joseph became second in command to Pharaoh, he started saving one-fifth of the food supply so that when the famine came, Egypt and the surrounding lands survived. Keep in mind that Joseph had seven good years to do that, and the famine lasted seven years. America and the world have had about fifty or sixty years of prosperity, only interrupted by short recessions. In the worst-case scenario, we may have less than seven years before an economic disaster unfolds, and any economic disaster may last longer than seven years.

The big question for believers is who wants to be ready to make a difference if something catastrophic happens? Will we be ready with our house in order? Will we have our debt under control, and will we have emergency savings? Will our expenses be down to a sustainable level? Egypt was ready because God guided Joseph to save Egypt and used him to save his own family.

Will we be ready for the greatest revival of all time involving our children?

7

CONCLUSION

THRIVING IN DISASTER, MISSION FOCUSED

Many models exist for surviving and even thriving in calamities and disasters. What helps some soldiers who fought in Iraq or Afghanistan endure while others come out severely wounded emotionally? What helped soldiers through the Vietnam War? How did the 442nd soldiers and the millions in WWII charge into probable death, be able to live through the day, and come out after the night? Why are some disabled by Post Traumatic Stress Disorder, while others come out stronger after going through disastrous events?

The God factor is the foundation, but I believe a clear and compelling mission can be the difference between thriving and crashing. Those who are willing to die for their mission have a stronger faith that helps them through the situation. It may be the difference between someone whose fears keep them from charging forward in a hail of bullets, and the one who charges. Both are afraid. Both fear death, yet one charges forward. If their mission is clear, they can charge forward.

I believe embracing God's original instructions for Adam as well as embracing God's main focus for us can help us thrive as we walk through any disaster, especially an economic one. The ability to thrive through our mission is enhanced by the stakes at hand, and there are no higher stakes than if this generation or the next is the last generation.

GOD'S INSTRUCTIONS TO ADAM: BE FRUITFUL

In Genesis 1:28, God instructed Adam "Be fruitful," while His second command was to "increase in number." The remaining commands were part of Adam's responsibilities and defined the authority that God gave Adam. He also gave Adam resources and work to do.

> God blessed them and said to them, "Be fruitful [MISSION] and increase in number [COMMAND]; fill the earth and subdue it [RESPONSIBILITY]. Rule over the fish of the sea and the birds of the air and over every living creature that moves on the ground [AUTHORITY]." Then God said, "I give you every seed-bearing plant on the face of the whole earth and every tree that has fruit with seed in it. They will be yours for food. And to all the beasts of the earth and all the birds of the air and all the creatures that move on the ground — everything that has the breath of life in it — I give every green plant for food [RESOURCES]." And it was so (Genesis 1:28-30 with personal comments).

> The Lord God took the man and put him in the Garden of Eden to work it and take care of it [WORK and WORSHIP] (Genesis 2:15).

Our mission, God's commands, our responsibility, authority, resources, work, and worship are foundational to our walk with God.

These aspects are all tied together and cannot be separated. Work, if done exclusively for God, is our spiritual act of worship (Romans 12:1).

GOD'S ULTIMATE DESIRE IS FOR US TO BECOME LIKE JESUS

The Bible covers so much ground that we can get lost in the depth of its goodness. As I think about principles that can guide me towards eternity, I try to develop a concept to follow. Here are four interrelated truths:

1. God's ultimate desire is for us to "become like His Son" (Romans 8:29, NLT).
2. God calls us to a mission by giving us a cause that completes us. We will always be lacking if we do not connect with our cause. We can become like Jesus as long as we keep walking in our mission.
3. His command to be fruitful can only be accomplished if we "become like His Son."

God's plan is for us to walk with Him as we serve in our mission. God walks with us, strengthens us, guides us, empowers us, and helps us to grow so we can become like Jesus and bear fruit. The mission is important because it helps us to keep going, as we know that we are sent by God. As we continue our walk, God imparts His faith to us.

You may have a different and better model, but in my model, doing the work God assigns to me helps me to become like Jesus. God's ultimate desire for me is about *being* not doing, although both are important. I would not try to separate one from the other, for they exist to complement each other. I need to do what Christ wants in order to become like Christ, and I need to become like Christ in order to effectively do the "good things he planned for us long ago" (Ephesians 2:10, NLT).

I know that for me, I reach different levels of fruitfulness as I depend on the grace of God. God has blessed me abundantly, but I realize that my measure of fruitfulness is different from God's view of fruitfulness for me. I can think that I am doing much for him, but God's view could be different. "If you did it my way, I could multiply your work a hundredfold. You think you are doing a lot, by now you should be doing much more. You are doing the work of a baby, by now you should be doing the work of a man. If you depended on me, the Holy Spirit would have sent you an army to do the work. If you had faith in me, and you waited on me, I would have showed up a week later and done great and marvelous things. Instead, you are satisfied with the heavy lifting of the work of your hands. And you are proud of it."

WE ARE PRONE TO HAVING THE WRONG FOCUS

I sometimes think I focus on the work I do for God too much, which can make it harder to become like Jesus. I should not just sit down, but I should work and serve Him diligently. Our Lord, our Savior, the Creator of all things, and the One Who gives all good things deserves no less. Somewhere hidden in my heart lies a key that can unlock the kingdom of heaven within me. That key is tied to who gets the glory as I work and serve. Who looks good as I do my work for Him?

If I secretly think that I want someone to recognize my work, I can only receive that recognition from my fellow man. If I do not reach my goals or the goals that someone sets for me, I am prone to becoming anxious. I can very easily get angry and distressed. I keep thinking that someone will measure what I am doing and think that I am falling short. In that state of mind, it does not matter if God thinks I have been completely fruitful. I fail to view success from God's view. Maybe He thinks I became a little like Jesus that day. I need to stop and ask, "Lord are you still pleased with the work of my hands?" My concern is often, "What will others think? What will they say? Do they know what happened?" I know that Jesus "did not need man's testimony about man, for he knew what was in man" (John 2:25). Since I am woefully stuck in my performance-oriented view of service to God, when I fail to accomplish what I set out to do, I do not allow Jesus' words to give me peace when there are men and women around to measure me.

As I walk on the path God laid out for me, I think I have a better chance of becoming like Jesus if I focus on the following things that are important to Jesus.

1. **God the Father** and all that goes along with Him, including obedience, faith, hope, and love. Evangelism is at the heart of God the Father. "Now this is eternal life: that they may know you, the only true God, and Jesus Christ, whom you have sent" (John 17:3).

2. **Revelation and dependence on the Holy Spirit**. After all Jesus left us the Spirit.

3. **Family** is important since it is part of the hundredfold blessing. "'I tell you the truth,' Jesus replied, 'no one who has left home or brothers or sisters or mother or father or children or fields for me and the gospel will fail to receive a hundred times as much in this present age (homes, brothers, sisters, mothers, children and fields — and with them, persecutions) and in the age to come, eternal life'" (Mark 10:29-30).

4. **God is love,** and He wants us to love.

These are my four priority focuses that help me to become like Jesus. You may have your own list, and you would do well to shoot for your own targets. As I walk my mission, if I keep these in mind, I might move up the ladder a little each year. I know God will not give up on me, as He has "predestined [us] to become conformed to the image of His Son" (Romans 8:29, NKJV).

As I obey God's instructions in some of the other areas, I must try to keep in mind these four focus areas: the Father, the Holy Spirit, family, and love. God will help me become like Jesus if I keep my eyes on these four areas, as well as walk in the various commands and plans that He gives to me.

GO, BECOME LIKE JESUS, AND BEAR FRUIT

Salvation is the work of God; sanctification is the work of God. I am not pushing Calvinism, in which we do not need to go. God uses us when we go. Let us look at a couple of passages.

"No one can come to me unless the Father who sent me draws him, and I will raise him up at the last day" (John 6:44). Jesus tells us no one can come to him unless the Father draws that person so I see that God is working through the Holy Spirit in each person's life.

In Philippians 2:13, we see that "it is God who works" in people to "will and to act according to his good purposes."

Going to make disciples is a command that God gave us and should be taken seriously. Some do this aggressively; some do not do it even passively. Whatever we do, God moves us towards becoming like Jesus, which then results in us bearing fruit.

I remember an early episode when I was with Daven, and we went to an early morning surf session with one of his friends, Chris. We were just about ready to enter the water when I noticed a guy sitting on the benches that I had seen a number of times before. I rushed back to my car to get one of my early Christian War Packets and gave it to him. He asked, "What's this?" I told him it was about God. He went berserk and started swearing and yelling. I calmly took back the War Packet and walked back to my car to save it for another. He kept yelling and cussing. As we entered the water, Chris said, "Uncle Jimmy, I think he misunderstood you." I just smiled at Chris, and we paddled out. I realized then that I had no animosity towards the man, and more importantly, I was making disciples of my kids. I had failed in evangelism, but I passed the *agape* test. My results with regards to the stranger were not fruitful, and while Daven does not remember any of the waves he caught that day, he remembers the episode.

Bearing fruit is not about making lots of disciples and a few enemies along the way. Bearing fruit brings God's love into every situation, whether we are participating in evangelism, serving, teaching, or correcting. We allow God to do the work.

THRIVING BY BECOMING LIKE JESUS – FAMILY STYLE

I believe that my kids (and your kids) are part of what I call the "Absolute Greatest Generation," because they have the greatest mission, which has the highest and most important stakes. As I presented earlier, I believe the Bible makes a case for Jesus' return possibly within this generation, or the next. While this may or may not be correct, what is true is that Christianity rests on the shoulders of the next generation. If we do not hand off our faith properly and we fumble away the opportunity here today, Christianity may die. Of course, God is in control and that will not happen, but we must play our part.

As I layout the priority structure of God first, wife and kids second, work and ministry third and fourth (and some reverse this order), it seems to me that the developing of our kids as missionaries, marketplace ministers, marketplace evangelists, marketplace teachers, etc., should be my top priority. I believe the most effective way for this to take place is satisfy God's desire for me to become like Jesus, love my kids, and help them as much as I can in their job, walk, and ministry.

This means we support Jason, give him responsibility and authority to run A-1 A-Lectrician, are there if he falters, and support him when he has issues. This means we support Daven in his ministry, babysit on a regular schedule, do not get upset when they do not make our family functions, encourage him in his short comings, and help him in his issues and struggles. This means even though I think he should be in the Word more, I do not push it, which is hard. This means we support Lisa in her desire to build a print media mini empire, love the people she loves, love the work she is doing, and express to her, "Lisa, there is nothing you can do that will make Dad love you less."

As we raise the next generation, although I recognize that education is important, reading and studying God's Word are important, finding a job is important, building savings, home, and family are important, and going and making disciples are important, all of these areas are not the ultimate desires of God for them. I set as my goal to help them become the person that God wants them to be, which is to become like Jesus. I can talk about this and can even write a book about this and give it to them for their birthdays, but they would rather have money. The best thing is to walk with them as I try to set my heart on my becoming like Jesus, not working hard at getting them to become like Jesus. No amount of teaching or effort can help me accomplish that. Only God can help them to become like Jesus, and I hope He decides to use Diana and I.

I think that if they can become like Jesus, they will have the best shot at thriving in all disasters.

MAXIMUM EVANGELISM AND MAXIMUM MISSION

Once we can approach being the person Jesus wants us to be, we approach the sweet spot of evangelism effectiveness. Our spouses love us more, and our kids can see we love them unconditionally. Our workers and bosses love our work ethic, and the Holy Spirit maximizes drawing all people with whom you come into contact to Jesus. God also maximizes His impact and timing in conforming people to the "likeness of His Son" (Romans 8:29). People get saved and become more like Jesus. As we love unconditionally, God does the work through our love and actions.

The best part is that our kids will learn the way of *agape* and that will be the best preparation method for this group that God may one day say, "This is the Absolute Greatest Generation." Kids equipped with this method, surrounded by an army of *agape* warriors will have little difficulty thriving during difficult periods. Our job as parents, uncles, *hanai* family members, church family, work family, and even street family is to prepare them so they can be part of the Absolute Greatest Generation.

Jason's wife Donna came from Korea when she was about fifteen years old. Her two sisters were twelve and nine, and her brother was six. Their mother chose to stay in Korea so you can imagine the difficulties that the family had in America. Although they knew about God and their father was a believer, there was very little focus on becoming like Jesus. For the Paks, life was extremely difficult, and their growth in Christ was stymied very early.

After Jason and Donna were married in 2005, Donna grew spiritually. She was always the matriarch of her family, but now that she had found a new mom and dad in Diana and I, she really fulfilled her role as the matriarch of her family. Although her family is scattered across the United States from Las Vegas to New York and New Jersey, her family is more connected than many families that live in the same state. I attribute that to Jason and Donna becoming more like Jesus.

SATAN'S ONSLAUGHT GIVES US A HINT

Satan knows his time is short and that Jesus will return soon. Satan knows that this generation or the next or the one after that may be the Absolute Greatest, so he has pulled out all his stops and has been working twenty-four hours a day and seven days a week using all of his resources, including his evil angels as well as whoever he can possess or influence, to blind our kids and anyone around us that he can affect. I believe he has and is using the following and more.

1. Media, movies, television, and internet
2. The arts, pictures, books, and articles
3. Educational systems at all levels from early grade levels through universities
4. Political and governmental structures and systems
5. Medical fields, hospitals, and care homes
6. Businesses

I am not saying all of the above are evil but that Satan has influenced people in all of these areas and more. His purpose is to blind people so they cannot understand what believers are telling them about Jesus Christ (2 Corinthians 4:4).

SATAN HAS TARGETED THIS GENERATION

Children are easily influenced. Children's minds work well in regards to memory retention. Young babies can learn languages, gain an appreciation of music, and learn very quickly, and at an early age, they can manipulate and control their parents. They have the capacity to learn to read, write, speak, multiply, learn algebra, and understand the sciences *ad infinitum*.

Child sex offenders prey on children because they are easily influenced. However, children cannot comprehend a sex offender preying on them. The offender will build a relationship (90% know their targets), treat them well, give them gifts, and then ZAP! The kids do not know what hit them, and they are trapped.

Satan works the same way. He has access to kids' minds. He preys on kids, infiltrates their minds through music, movies, and television programs that activate their senses so that they delight in the sensual, which is very easy, considering the way God made boys and girls. If they are strong, he incites them to power. If they are leaders, he incites them to motivating and controlling people. If they are believers, He tells them, "It's okay; everyone is doing it. How can it be so wrong if it feels so good? Your parents don't want you to enjoy life. Don't you wish you could decide for yourself, good and evil, right and wrong? This is a new age. Your parents are dummies; look how people laugh at them on the television."

Satan communicates ideas to them that he has learned over the thousands of years he has been in existence. Satan is smarter and wiser than these kids.

EVEN JESUS RECOGNIZED SATAN'S EFFECTIVENESS

In the days before his crucifixion, Jesus said to his disciples, "Do you see all these things? I tell you the truth, not one stone here will be left on another; everyone will be thrown down." His disciples asked Jesus, "When will this happen, and what will be the sign of your coming and of the end of the age?" (Matthew 24:2-3).

Jesus told them a number of things to watch for and then said something very interesting, "Because of the increase of wickedness, the love [*agape*] of most will grow cold" (Matthew 24:12). I believe his main concern here was that the love of many of the believers would grow cold, due to the increase in wickedness. As I apply this to our kids, Satan will attack many of them, and they may fall into all kinds of wickedness, lawlessness, evil lifestyles, and iniquity. They may lie to us, steal from us, disappoint us if they get caught up in drugs and alcohol, and cause us to suffer distress and heartache.

Jesus did not change His new commandment that He gave to us in John 13:34. The commandment is the same for our kids, the same for our families, and the same for our co-workers and bosses:.love one another as He loved us. Jesus knows that when the proverbial "all hell is busting loose," in us is being a person with *agape* love. The most powerful act of evangelism for our kids to see. The most effective method of having a permanent impact on our kids' lives is living *agape*. The Holy Spirit can take that love and move in the hearts of our kids and touch them. Time is on our side. Do you have faith?

The main issue will not be the falling away of our kids into sin or their participation in wickedness. The main issue will be can God's believers stand strong in *agape* love and not let their kids' wretched behavior cause their love to grow cold? If we fail in this, our love was conditionally dependent on our kids' good behavior. Only if they stay on the straight and narrow, would we love them. After all, we think, "We brought them up right. They better end up good." This is not being the person God wants us to be.

THE MAIN GOAL IS TO BECOME LIKE JESUS AND THRIVE BY BEING

Anyone who shoots for God's desire to become like Jesus moves from the accomplishment mentality to the being mentality. He moves from doing to being. As we focus on being, we make it our goal to please God. Can I still have faith in God regardless of whether we prosper financially or not, whether we live or whether we die? Can we be at peace when all around us people are losing their minds in rage because of the evil done to them, especially by their kids?

Having faith in God does not mean the believer lives in a perpetual state of "Kumbaya" and does not suffer distress. Diana experiences her biggest challenges when something bad happens to our kids, whether from sin or due to natural emergencies. Diana may experience distress, but she does not react under duress because she wants to react with *agape*. She may feel like reacting without thinking, but she presses in and squeezes out *agape* from deep down because she is focused on becoming like Jesus. She starts cooking.

The believer may plan, encourage, pray, and weep, and these reactions are all part of *agape*. During trying times we apply one of our life verses.

When I shut up the heavens so that there is no rain, or command locusts to devour the land or send a plague among my people, if my people, who are called by my name, will humble themselves and pray and seek my face and turn from their wicked ways, then will I hear from heaven and will forgive their sin and will heal their land (2 Chronicles 7:13-14).

If we are to be fruitful in difficult situations, especially ones through which our kids or others put us and if we resolve to apply this verse to our time and situation, we might be able to thrive in disasters. I think this verse has the three most important uses of the word "and" in the Bible. Now I realize that some focus on one part of this verse and use it to call people to pray, humble themselves, and turn from their wicked ways, but I believe that the three uses of "and" join the four conditional phrases together and make them one.

I will add my own perspective. I want to apply this to living with our kids and others today. God says that when He brings hard times on people, believers or non-believers, for not living the way God desires, which will happen to our kids and others if they are living off track. God tells us the way back for all people. He asks His believers today to do four things.

1. Humble themselves
   AND
2. Pray
   AND
3. Seek His face
   AND
4. Turn from their wicked ways

God will hear our prayers, forgive our (believers') sin, and bring people back to Jesus. He does not ask for those off track to get on track. How can they? He asks the strong believers to have faith in Him for the healing that people need.

This verse focuses on us being people who do things pleasing to God, being humble, praying, seeking Him, and turning with the resulting healing of the land coming through the fruitfulness that God brings.

GOD HEALS THE LAND AS WE OBEY

Healing the land relates to the removal of the discipline God brings on the land due to the disobedience of believers living in the land, whether in our homes or America. As I apply this passage to believers today, I believe God brings discipline, possibly in the form of illness or economic disaster, as our nation has turned away from Him.

Let us examine the following important question: is God requiring all believers to participate in the three "ANDS" or just those who are standing strong like Elijah and the seven thousand in 1 Kings 19:18? I believe that God is saying only those that are truly standing strong in loving God and loving others are able to participate in the healing of their land. For those living this passage today, God can bring healing to their households, families, kids, workplaces, and even their communities where they live. God can also heal the whole land, state, or nation, and all will benefit, although only a few, who meet the three "ANDS" test, will receive the rewards in heaven. Others merely escape the flames (1 Corinthians 3:15).

The number of people meeting the three "ANDS" test is not crucial to God, but God does desire our unity. Jesus said, "Again, I tell you that if two of you on earth agree about anything you ask for, it will be done for you by my Father in heaven. For where two or three come together in my name, there am I with them" (Matthew 18:19-20).

John writes, "This is the confidence we have in approaching God: that if we ask anything according to his will, he hears us. And if we know that he hears us — whatever we ask — we know that we have what we asked of him" (1 John 5:14-15).

I believe that if God's people stand strong for Christ and live the three "ANDS," then at God's appointed time, God can heal our land, my house, my family, and my kids. This will require believers to live a life of *agape*, to be who God wants them to be, to humble themselves by not striking back at their kids, bosses, or workers, and to pray for God to bring salvation into their families. Believers need to pray for the souls of their kids and love them even if they may be backsliding. The goal is for me to be who God wants me to be, not to accomplish a change in my kids' or others' way of life and attitudes, trying to force them to live a godly life. As parents, we love to see that, but God is the One Who makes the change in them. He will use us being like Jesus to transform them.

Maybe our kids are not backsliding, but they are just living through difficult times because of the wickedness around them. God sent us as His hand with which to bring His love so that they can thrive. Maybe God is trying to help them become more like Jesus by telling us if we become like Jesus to them, they will become like Jesus to their families and others, one day in God's timing. Maybe our expectations for our kids are too high. Maybe God is showing His mercy through His *agape* and through our *agape* for them, walking with them through their disasters. What if all Christian families lived this way? Would God heal the whole land?

BEING OR PERFORMING: WHAT IS THE DIFFERENCE?

Being does not require performance. The person who is simply being still serves, works, studies to know God, reaches out in love, lives in love, and loves to live. God is the center of his life, and any work he does is for the Lord. The goal is different from one who is focused on performance and making things happen, although both do as much as they can. The scorecard has different metrics for the one focused on being the person God wants him to be. The one focused on doing measures himself by his victories, activities, ministries, what he did for God, and the changes he affected in people. The following are some examples of contrasting metrics.

1. The person focused on doing measures the length of his prayers. (There is nothing wrong with long prayers.) The being person prays, but he asks, "Has my relationship with God deepened? Did I hear from God? Was God pleased? Did God speak to me?" The doing person prays to God, and he asks, "Did God deliver? Did God move? Did God answer the prayer in the manner I wanted?" If not, he feels disappointed. The being person is not disappointed because he knows God hears his prayers and is satisfied. He trusts God to act when He wants, how He wants, and if He wants. Our metrics are an important way to measure whether we are using the right model.

2. The person who is focused on doing counts how many he reached (although there is nothing wrong with this). The being person reaches out also, but he tries to listen to God who directs him to people he is to reach. He wants to hear from God. Is his walk on the mark or one inch off? He desires to be on the mark. He relishes God's correction. Whether he touches one or one hundred, his question is, "Did I hear from God?" The person focused on doing measures service to God by success in numbers.

3. The person focused on doing asks, "How many came to the Lord this week and this year?" The being person lets his life be his gospel. He uses words if he must. He knows God is drawing people to him, so he waits on God for direction: who, what, how, and when should he be? The person focused on doing needs metrics.

4. Both those focused on being and doing work hard and serve with all their strength. However, one is anxious, and one is not. One worries; one trusts. One counts; one does not. One must work hard; one lives by faith because that is who he is. One gets a little angry when people do not do as much as he does; one loves God and thanks Him for the abilities given to him and loves to help others reach their potential, whatever that is. One gets frustrated when he does not reach his goals; one lets God set his goals. One lives by the law; one lives by grace.

For both, the Holy Spirit can move, a mighty revival can break out, and God can heal the land. But only one believer's family thrives, even in turmoil. I do not know which one you are, but I know which one I want to be.

THE POWER OF THE FAMILY: THRIVING THROUGH A SOLID FAMILY CULTURE

CAN A FAMILY CREATE A TIPPING POINT?

The Tipping Point: How Little Things Can Make a Big Difference by Malcolm Gladwell describes how sociological changes can take place quickly. Gladwell defines these changes as tipping points. He uses many examples of these types of changes: New York crime, Paul Revere's ride, as well as evangelist John Wesley, and the start of the Methodist denomination.

Gladwell describes three rules: the Law of the Few, the Stickiness Factor, and the Power of Context. He also expands on the role the Law of the Few plays in the tipping point. Connectors, Mavens, and Salesmen characterize the Law of the Few. Connectors are those in the community who know large numbers of people and act as social hubs. Mavens are information specialists who also love to help people. Salesmen are persuasive, charismatic people who have tremendous abilities to influence others.

Under the Power of Context, Gladwell highlights the theory of the Broken Window.

> [It] was the brainchild of the criminologists James Q. Wilson and George Kelling. [They] argued that crime is the inevitable result of disorder. If a window is broken and left unrepaired, people walking by will conclude that no one cares and no one is in charge… minor problems like graffiti, public disorder, aggressive panhandling… are the equivalent of broken windows, invitations to more serious crimes: [in this environment] muggers and robbers… believe they reduce their chances of being caught… where potential victims are already intimidated by prevailing conditions…

> This is an epidemic theory of crime. It says crime is contagious… it can start with a broken window and spread to an entire community. The Tipping Point in this epidemic, though, isn't a particular person… The impetus to engage in a certain kind of behavior is not coming from a certain kind of person but from a feature of the environment.[1]

This is the Power of Context: the environment we live in has a huge impact on the way we respond in life. Gladwell references another study done in the early 1970s where a group of

> social scientists at Stanford University, led by Philip Zimbardo, decided to create a mock prison in the basement of the university's psychology building. The purpose of the experiment was to try to find out why prisons are such nasty places. Was it full of nasty people, or was it because prisons are such nasty environments that they make people nasty?

The result of the study was the impact on normal people who volunteered for guards and prisoners.

As the experiment progressed, the guards got systematically crueler and more sadistic. [Zimbardo] was shocked at the intensity of the change and the speed at which it happened.

One of the prisoners said after the experiment was over, "that no matter how together I thought I was inside my head, my prisoner behavior was often less under my control than I realized."

Zimbardo's conclusion was that there are specific situations so powerful that they can overwhelm our inherent predispositions. The key word here is situation. Zimbardo isn't talking about environment, but about the major external influences and situations that impact our lives: parents, schools, friends, and neighborhoods. His point is simply that there are certain times and places and conditions when much of that can be swept away, that there are instances where you can take normal people… and powerfully affect their behavior merely by changing the immediate details of their situation.[2]

The change in situation becomes their Tipping Point.

THE TIPPING POINT AND THE PATTERNS AND LAWS OF GOD

God has physical, social, scientific, and spiritual laws. Physical laws affect our bodies, such as our health when we exercise. Social laws affect our emotions and relationships. Scientific laws affect atoms, the earth, air, and water. Spiritual laws affect man and his relationship with God, man's actions and consequences.

God tells us that He causes all things to work together for our good (Romans 8:28). Most of the time, how He is working is not obvious to us. A fisherman looking into the ocean for fish watches for patterns in the ocean and sky. If he sees birds, he knows there are fish nearby. If the birds are flying high, he knows the fish are deep. If the birds are diving, he knows the fish are feeding at the surface. Like the fisherman, we can look for patterns that repeat, and when we see them, God could be fishing for something, maybe us. God is working for good. He does so in consistent ways that we can see His hand moving, but we need to be looking.

I will touch upon a few verses that reveal God's spiritual and social laws, which are all essentially God's laws of the universe.

> For if you live according to the sinful nature, you will die; but if by the Spirit you put to death the misdeeds of the body, you will live (Romans 8:13).

> And we know that in all things God works for the good of those who love him… (Romans 8:28).

> He who believes in me will live, even though he dies; and whoever lives and believes in me will never die. Do you believe this? (John 11:25-26).

> the Lord disciplines those he loves, and he punishes everyone he accepts as a son (Hebrews 12:6).

> The Lord God said, "It is not good for the man to be alone. I will make a helper suitable for him (Genesis 2:18).

PRACTICAL APPLICATIONS OF GOD'S PATTERNS

The following are some patterns in life where we can practically see God repeating His work for good in our lives.

1. God wants me to be prepared. Pattern - When I'm not prepared, God shows up.

2. God wants us to see the signs of the times that He sends. Pattern - If I am not aware, He hits me on the head and in my heart.

3. God wants me to be prepared. Pattern - God prepares my family for my benefit.

4. God wants me to be fruitful. Pattern - He guides my steps to get me to my mission. As I walk that mission, He helps me become fruitful.

5. God makes my mission clear. Pattern - He walks with me to get me to see my mission.

6. God works in the economy suddenly. Pattern - Watch for sudden events because God is there.

7. God impacts our pocketbooks to get our attention. Pattern - God cuts holes in our pockets.

8. God will always help us build our families. Pattern - He walks with us so that we can walk with them. Our families have trouble so that we will walk with them.

9. God orchestrates economic cycles and long stock market cycles. When God blesses, people indulge in pleasure. God brings correction cycles through market corrections. If governments try to negate these corrections, the eventual market correction is even greater, since governments are fighting against God's correction. This cycle is the pattern we see in the book of Judges. Pattern - Watch for an economic disaster to appear.

10. God is working for our good. Pattern - watch for the good in your life. Look back, and you will see God's hand.

These are some of the broad patterns. God is more involved than we have seen, but not more than His Word tells us. You may recognize different patterns that are obvious to you, or you may need to look for the less obvious patterns.

GOD'S TRUTH PATTERNS

Many of the laws of God are truths He wrote through the prophets. Many are clear like those in Romans 8:13, John 11:25, and
Genesis 2:18. God knows it is not good for man to be alone because
He made us, and we were made for relationships, first with Him but
also between ourselves.

The Tipping Point concept in relation to the Power of Context
as explained by Gladwell is an application of one of God's laws concerning community. Gladwell looks through secular lenses, but he
sees God's laws working in the world.

The way a person lives in his specific environment and circumstances causes that person to revert back to his base sinful nature: he
is prone to lust, cravings, and pride, and even reacts against his belief
system. Regardless of a person's belief system, his sinful nature is so
powerful that it can rule him. He can react disobediently, since God
turned us over to disobedience (Romans 11:32). He can act wick-
edly if thrown into a disastrous situation with extreme stress. He
can react proudly and arrogantly even if he has seen the wondrous
works of God just as Hezekiah foolishly showed off his riches in Isaiah
39:4-7. This may explain why kids who move away to college follow
the crowd. Their belief system short-circuits if it is not solidly rooted
in their soul; the pressure of the situation through the other students'
activities cause them to crash. If the Holy Spirit is strong in their
lives, they bounce back. If not, they have a long road ahead.

The importance of environment explains the powerful move of
God in the community in the Book of Acts.

> They devoted themselves to the apostles' teaching and
> to the fellowship, to the breaking of bread and to prayer.
> Everyone was filled with awe, and many wonders and
> miraculous signs were done by the apostles. All the believ-
> ers were together and had everything in common. Selling

their possessions and goods, they gave to anyone as he had need. Every day they continued to meet together in the temple courts. They broke bread in their homes and ate together with glad and sincere hearts, praising God and enjoying the favor of all the people. And the Lord added to their number daily those who were being saved (Acts 2:42-47, NIV).

This passage explains the result of the Holy Spirit coming upon the believers just after the Day of Pentecost. A community formed which nurtured believers to be fruitful. All the essential elements that embodied community were present including teaching, fellowship, prayer, and breaking of bread for Holy Communion as well as meals. No one needed to force the believers to stay together. No one needed to preach about sharing and giving. No one forced them to meet daily. They ate in their homes together with joy, worship, and praise, and even unbelievers liked their new neighbors. They were fruitful, loved God, and loved others. "The Lord added... daily those who were being saved." Community was a powerful tipping point for unity among the early believers.

God says "it is not good for man to be alone." We know that when believers react so that people can see the love of God in community, people know they are not alone. In *The Tipping Point*, we saw the impact that situations and local conditions can have on a person's reaction and adaptation to his context environment.

The example of the community of early believers fits with Gladwell's conclusions and shows us that any community that has *agape* love and includes fellowship, prayer, and God's teaching on how to obey Jesus, and shares food and needs, will thrive no matter the circumstances. The reaction of the people in the surrounding community will be powerfully affected by the *agape* love of the believers as they emulate Christ. This is what being fruitful is all about.

I believe that Gladwell recognized a God-ordained pattern whereby a community of people can impact those around them very powerfully, for their good or for their destruction. We as believers can use this pattern to work for us, if we can create a strong community that looks like Jesus within our families. A family living like the book of Acts with *agape* love as the basis for being can have a strong long-term impact on the lives of their kids.

Those in an *agape* community do not react with bitterness or anger when someone fails. They do not react in anger saying, "How could you do that? Didn't you know? How could you hurt me like that? I told you a thousand times not to do that. That's it. I'm out of here. I've had it with you."

A dad, mom, son, or daughter reacting in love would say, "What you did was wrong, yet there is nothing you can do that would make me love you less. I'll pray for you. How can I help you? Are you hungry? Let's eat."

In an *agape* community such as a church or non-profit, if someone violated the rules of the program, the loving reaction would be, "There is nothing you can do that would make me love you less. However, what you did was wrong, and I have to remove you from leadership or the program."

In a business, a loving response would be, "I love you but our policy is zero tolerance for drug use, so I have to fire you. Hope to see you at Bible study."

The key point is that whether we are using God's Word or the secular principles of *The Tipping Point*, we must recognize that the power of the community can move a person to wickedness and evil, or towards repentance, love, and back to the lordship of Christ. Using Zimbardo's conclusion again, "there are specific situations so powerful that they can overwhelm our inherent predispositions."

Situations may be recognizable as patterns where God allows people to fall into disobedience, which may reveal to them their own wickedness. Once they know they are forgiven much, they can love God much. God could also be testing and strengthening our *agape* love in our families and communities to build powerful places where hurting souls can experience firsthand the risen Lord through us as we take up our cross. We can all become more like Jesus as we walk together through these situations with God. Then we will bring transformation to our communities as we become like the church in the Book of Acts.

JESUS' GAME PLAN TO THRIVE THROUGH BEING

COMING AFTER JESUS

Jesus laid out a very simple plan for his disciples. "Then Jesus said to his disciples, 'If anyone would come after me, he must deny himself and take up his cross and follow me'" (Matthew 16:24). This statement can be spoken in seven seconds and memorized in one minute but takes a lifetime to live. I believe Jesus gave us the model for becoming like Him and being fruitful.

JESUS' GAME PLAN FOR PETER – FOLLOW ME TO BECOME LIKE ME

Let us examine the last conversation in the Book of John.

When they had finished eating, Jesus said to Simon Peter, "Simon son of John, do you truly love me more than these?"

"Yes, Lord," he said, "you know that I love you."

Jesus said, "Feed my lambs."

Again Jesus said, "Simon son of John, do you truly love me?"

He answered, "Yes, Lord, you know that I love you."

Jesus said, "Take care of my sheep."

The third time he said to him, "Simon son of John, do you love me?"

Peter was hurt because Jesus asked him the third time, "Do you love me?" He said, "Lord, you know all things; you know that I love you."

Jesus said, "Feed my sheep. I tell you the truth, when you were younger you dressed yourself and went where you wanted; but when you are old you will stretch out your hands, and someone else will dress you and lead you where you do not want to go." Jesus said this to indicate the kind of death by which Peter would glorify God. Then he said to him, "Follow me!" (John 21:15-19).

Most of you know the story. Peter had failed Jesus by denying him three times, something he never expected to do. He thought he loved Jesus so much he would die for him if needed. When Jesus came to Peter and asked three times if Peter loved Him, Peter already knew he did not really love Jesus with an *agape* love like Jesus desired. The first two times, Jesus asked Peter if his love for Jesus was unconditional. Peter responded truthfully without boasting, and he recognized his love was only *phileo* love, or that of a friend. When Jesus asked the third time, "Peter, you're only my friend?" Peter was hurt, but it was the truth. Jesus recognized Peter was not yet the person He wanted him to be so Jesus instructed, "Feed my lambs… Take care of my sheep… Feed my sheep."

GOD HELPS US BECOME LIKE JESUS

In his book *That None Should Perish*, Ed Silvoso explains that he writes as a practitioner, not as a biblical scholar.[3] If it's good for Ed Silvoso, it's good for me. As you read the following paragraphs, recognize that this is not a complete theological explanation but a means of explaining how I apply these passages to my life.

Jesus previously said to his disciples, "If anyone would come after me, he must deny himself and take up his cross and follow me"

(Matthew 16:24). I see the same principle in what Jesus told Peter in John 21 as Jesus gives specific instructions consistent with His earlier teaching. Jesus realized Peter wanted to follow Him in *agape* love but was not yet at the *agape* love level. Jesus was telling Peter, "It's okay. I know you don't have an *agape* love for me. You ran away from me because when you were young, you had bad habits. You did what you wanted to do. You wanted what you wanted. You wanted things your way.

"But if you keep on feeding my lambs even when it is difficult, if you keep on taking care of my sheep, if you keep on feeding my sheep and daily giving them food, water, clothing, or whatever they need, then the Holy Spirit will work in you to help you to be who I want you to be. You will become like me. Stop doing things your way and practice denying yourself by serving my sheep. You have twenty years of bad habits that are hard to break. Now that you are saved, work out your salvation, and practice denying yourself.

"As you grow by denying yourself, you will soon graduate to taking up your cross, and you will gladly die for my sheep. You will continue to grow and become a leader, but don't get too proud because if you do, you will start to be more concerned about what people think about you. When I initially sent you, I did the miraculous through you, and you became proud saying, 'Lord, even the demons submit to us in your name' (Luke 10:17). But don't worry, I'll send Paul to reprimand you" (Galatians 2:11-21).

"As you continue to take up your cross, I'll lead you to higher and higher mountains, and since you will be filled with the Holy Spirit, one day you will not even care what men think. At that point, you will have only my Heart at the center of your heart and you will only want what I want for you. When you reach that point, you will stretch out your hands, and you will truly follow me. You're not there yet, but if you keep on serving people who are wretched, sinful, and evil, you will grow and suffer for my sake. The Holy Spirit will help you. The Holy Spirit will fill you with power, but don't let that go to your head. I know you, Peter.

"Don't be dismayed that you are only my friend at this point in time. I love you the way you are. I want you to become like me. I will guide you and help you. You will then love God with all your heart, soul, mind, and strength, and love others as I have loved you. You will then follow me, and I will be proud that you will *agape* me."

MY APPLICATION

In Chapter Four, I shared how I practiced denying myself certain delights. These were not sinful delights, but the focus was on practicing. We must flee sin so I'm not talking about sinful delights. The Apostles Paul and Peter were filled with the Holy Spirit in a powerful way and may not have needed practice, but I do. As I look back on my practice of denying myself things that delighted my senses, such as shrimp tempura and any sensual sights, I realize that this discipline helped me grow spiritually, and over the years, I continued practicing.

As I grow from denying myself to taking up my cross, and as the focus shifts from me to others, I find it easier to follow Christ. Note the God's pattern of change in focus: my focus shifts from me, to others, to Christ. Remember, I am writing as a practitioner, not a scholar.

I am not talking about a sequential exercise, where we practice denying for two years and then move up. I liken the spiritual exercise to the physical exercise of a football player and his workout routine. He bench presses to build muscle. He runs to improve his cardiovascular health. He practices his blocking or catching skills and plays in the football game on the weekend. He trains all week, and his training becomes part of who he is. Each exercise, each routine, including the big game, benefits the other routines. So it is with what Jesus is teaching. When we go and minister and serve someone, we practice denying, picking up our cross, and following Jesus, all simultaneously. We can also practice each spiritual discipline individually and increase the weight and intensity of the routine, especially as we depend on the Holy Spirit's guidance, power, and presence.

As I graduated to practicing taking up my cross in small areas, such as washing the dishes for my wife, loving my kids through their idiosyncrasies, and reaching out to the unlovable with no expectation of gain, I grew a little more spiritually. I still have a long journey, but I can look back on small victories and rejoice in them. I do not feel like God measures the amount of work, the size of the victories, or the quality of transformation in those I reach. I believe He recognizes those details as His responsibility. My metric has been, "am I being fruitful? Am I becoming the person He wants me to be?" When I practice washing dishes for Diana, am I doing it for God, even if she does not recognize me. When I practice not reacting to my kids' idiosyncrasies, I can discipline myself to trust God to mold them. I ask myself, "Am I obeying the command He gave me to love them as He loved me?" When I teach, preach, and minister, am I anxious because the quality of the transformation is not what I expect, in the lives of people in whom I invest?

What does it mean to take up my cross? Should I not expect change if I invest time and energy? When I look at Jesus, I do not see Him being anxious, nervous, or angry at the speed of my transformation. He was not anxious when I was six, twenty-two, or thirty-five years old. He had already done His work on the cross. He knew it was the Holy Spirit's role to draw me to Him (John 6:44). Once I came to Jesus on June 6, 1993, Jesus still was not anxious, nervous, or angry at my slow growth. He knew it was the role of the Holy Spirit to help me and to mold me. It is by grace. He doesn't use force. He is patient and waits for me to grow. If it's good for Jesus, it's good for me. As I apply this concept to my family and others, maybe one day, I can please God and become a little like Jesus. I might then maximize my fruitfulness in some of the things I do, and maybe even thrive.

MY METRIC FOR BECOMING LIKE JESUS

One of my dysfunctions is that I need metrics to challenge me to improve, so I have two metrics that I have targeted to help me in my quest. I am not talking about my mission and my call. I am talking about a means to measure internally how I am doing.

First, I set a goal that anytime I feel my blood pressure rising, my temperature heating up, my heart beating, or my mouth ready to attack, I resolve to seek God. "Oh God, oh God, oh God," I call on him out loud or in my mind. Once I start, my goal is not to stop until all my gauges reverse: my blood pressure, temperature, heart, and mouth need to go back to normal mode. Sometimes it take a few seconds, sometimes a few minutes, or sometimes hours for my soul to eventually reset to normal.

I started practicing crying out to God a number of years ago. My first trial run was when I slammed my finger in my car door. Rather than swearing like I normally did, I cried out, "Oh God, oh God, oh God," and held my finger. I also asked Him to heal my finger, while I continued calling out. "Success!" I thought. Since then, I used every painful moment as an opportunity to grow, and God was gracious to give me tons of them. For some reason, possibly due to old age, I seem to bump parts of my body into things in the world around me. I stub my toes against doorways, hit my shoulder against the walls, and bang my head against objects under which I bend. All this makes for a lot of practice.

The bigger tests are with the one I love the most, Diana. These tests do not happen too often, but I am tested when we disagree on something, mostly small, and she makes a comment that is really small. However, in my heart, the comment seems huge and hurtful. At other times, although this is rare, Diana may get upset about something that I preached or something that I did, and she eventually blows steam. On other occasions, Diana may criticize me for something small all because she loves me and because God made her different. During these eruptions, I try to go to God immediately and cry out, "Oh God, oh God, oh God." I do not do anything fancy, nor do I make special prayer requests. I just call to Him and cling to Him until the volcano inside me cools, and it always does.

The second goal that I shoot for is the "one millisecond rule." If I feel my volcano rising, my goal is to call on His name within one millisecond. As long as I call on God before my mouth reacts, things always work out because calling on God prevents me from saying anything stupid. As we all know, wisdom is generally lacking in moments when you are under attack or under duress. When my volcano is rising, I know I have evil within me, and I know that I have never said anything wise or uplifting to Diana in those moments. Zipping my mouth works best. I am shooting for one millisecond in every encounter, but I am not there yet.

Calling on God helps me prepare to thrive in any disaster, and I know many disasters are out there, and they are coming.

LESSON FROM DIETRICH BONHOEFFER, THE ULTIMATE EXAMPLE IN BEING LIKE JESUS AND FOLLOWING CHRIST

The invisible hand of God always moved Dietrich Bonhoeffer in tough situations, but Bonhoeffer trusted God completely to work everything out for good (Romans 8:28). Can trusting God unto death allow us to thrive? Did Bonhoeffer thrive, or was he fooling himself? Judge for yourself.

THE ULTIMATE TEST: TO BECOME LIKE CHRIST IN DEATH

One of the great men of faith is Dietrich Bonhoeffer. He was born in 1906 to Karl and Paula Bonhoeffer. They were a very well-to-do family and had a rich family lineage that traced back centuries. The

Dietrich Bonhoeffer

following biographical summary is drawn from an excellent book, *Bonfoeffer: Pastor, Martyr, Prophet, Spy* by Eric Metaxas.

Paula's "parents and family were closely connected to the emperor's court at Potsdam. Her aunt Pauline became a lady-in-waiting to Crown Princess Victoria, wife of Frederick III. Her father, Karl Alfred von Hase, had been a military chaplain to Kaiser Wilhem II. Her maternal side included artist and musicians… they included a painters… military aristocrats… and were socially and intellectually prominent Yorck von Wartenburgs."[4]

Karl Bonhoeffer's lineage was also impressive. "The family traced itself to 1403 in the annals of Nymwegen on the Waal River in the Netherlands, near the German border. In 1513, Caspar van den Boenhoff left the Netherlands to settle in the German city of Schwabisch Hall. The family was afterward called Bonhoffer… The Bonhoeffers were among the first families of Schwabisch Hall for three centuries. The earliest generations were goldsmiths; later generations included doctors, pastors, judges, professors, and lawyers. Through the centuries, 78 council members and three mayors in Schwabisch Hall were Bonhoeffers.[5]

"Napoleon's invasion in 1806 ended the free status of Schwabisch Hall and scattered the family... Karl Bonhoeffer's father, Friedrich Ernst Philipp Tobias Bonhoeffer (1828-1907), was a high ranking judiciary official throughout Wurttemberg, and ended his career as president of the Provincial Count in Ulm... The family trees of Karl and Paula Bonhoeffer are so laden with figures of accomplishment that one might expect future generations to be burdened by it all..."[6] His brother, "Karl-Friedrich landed a prestigious research position at the Kaiser Wilhelm Institute, where he would soon split the atom, absurdly raising the already high bar of accomplishment for his siblings..."[7]

When Dietrich turned fourteen and was ready to tell his family of his plan to be a theologian, he required boldness and courage that may have caused most normal kids to shrink back. "His father might treat it with respect...even if he disagreed, but his brothers and sister and their friends would not." Yet, Dietrich was no ordinary young man, and he stood his ground and made his choice.[8]

In 1939, Dietrich had a decision to make. He needed to register for the military, but he knew he could not serve in the German Army. He could not declare himself a conscientious objector so his hand was forced. After much prayer and discussion with his close friends, he decided to leave Germany, and he initiated a move to connect with Henry Leiper in New York, which allowed him to teach at Union Theological Seminary. On June 12, 1939, Dietrich "entered the great harbor of America for the second time... Henry Leiper met him for breakfast... He had not been in New York for 24 hours, but Bonhoeffer was already deeply out of sorts. He was sure that he must go back.[9]

"On June 20th, he had lunch with Henry Leiper, who set up the whole job and move opportunity to America. Dietrich wrote in his diary: 'The decision (to go back to Germany) had been made. I have refused. They were clearly disappointed, and rather upset. It probably means more for me than I can see at the moment. God alone knows what.'[10]

"Years later, Leiper recalled their lunch meeting there… 'What was my surprise and dismay to learn from my guest that he had just received an urgent appeal from his colleagues in Germany to return at once for important tasks which they felt he alone could perform…' he was determined to obey God and was sure he was doing so in deciding to return to Germany. He knew that the consequences of his obedience were God's business.[11]

Dietrich returned to Germany and participated in the plot to kill Hitler, providing much needed guidance to the generals and officers leading the plot. Metaxas writes, "No one has better attempted to explain the seeming paradox of a Christian involved in a plot to assassinate a head of state than (his good friend) Eberhard Bethge. He helps show that Bonhoeffer's steps toward political resistance were not some unwarranted detour from his previous thinking, but were a natural outworking of that thinking."[12]

Metaxas continues, "Bethge explained: '…We now realized that mere confession, no matter how courageous, inescapably meant complicity with the murderers… we were resisting by way of confession, but we were not confessing by way of resistance.'[13]

"A major theme for Bonhoeffer was that every Christian must be 'fully human' by bringing God into his whole life, not merely into some 'spiritual' realm. To be an ethereal figure who merely talked about God, but somehow refused to get his hands dirty in the real world, was bad theology."[14]

Eventually Dietrich Bonhoeffer was arrested and taken to Flossenburg prison where he was hanged two weeks before the Allied

Flossenburg Camp where Bonhoeffer was executed

forces liberated Flossenburg on April 23, 1945. The camp doctor at Flossenburg was H. Fischer-Hullstrung.[15]

Metaxas writes, "He had no idea who he was watching at the time, but years later, he gave the following account of Bonhoeffer's last minutes alive.[16]

'On the morning of that day between five and six o'clock the prisoners, among them Admiral Canaris, General Oster... were taken from their cells, and the verdicts of the court martial read out to them. Through the half-open door in one room of the huts I saw Pastor Bonhoeffer, before taking off his prison garb, kneeling on the floor praying fervently to his God. I was most deeply moved by the way this loveable man prayed, so devout and so certain that God heard his prayer. At the place of execution, he again said a short prayer and then climbed the steps to the gallows, brave and composed. His death ensued after a few seconds. In the almost fifty years that I worked as a doctor, I have hardly ever seen a man die so entirely submissive to the will of God.'"[17]

Metaxas continues, "Bonhoeffer thought of death as the last station on the road to freedom." Metaxas quotes a message that Dietrich preached in London. **"No one has yet believed in God and the kingdom of God, no one has yet heard about the realm of the resurrected, and not been homesick from that hour, waiting and looking forward joyfully to being released from bodily existence.**[18]

"Whether young or old makes no difference. What are twenty or thirty or fifty years in the sight of God? **... life only really begins when it ends here on earth,** that all that is here is only the prologue before the curtain goes up-that is for young and old alike to think about. Why are we so afraid when we think about death? ... Death is only dreadful for those who live in dread and fear of it... Death is grace, the greatest gift of grace that God gives to people who believe in him...[19]

"How do we know that dying is so dreadful? Who knows whether, in our human fear and anguish we are only shivering and shuddering at the most glorious, heavenly, blessed event in the world?"[20]

Surely, Dietrich Bonhoeffer followed Christ. Surely, he became like Christ. Surely, he thrived as he rode to Flossenburg and as he walked those last steps to the gallows. Surely, he thrived as he was hanged. Surely, he thrived as he took his last breath. Surely, he thrived when he saw his Lord "in the twinkling of an eye" (1 Corinthians 15:52).

Surely, none of us prefer to die, but dying for Christ may be a necessary part of living fully for Him. His words seem to say so, but sadly, those are only words to many.

BONHOEFFER'S BELIEFS

Strong beliefs do not guarantee that strong Christians will follow Christ in every aspect of living, especially during difficult moments. Nevertheless, let us take a close look at some of Bonhoeffer's beliefs.

Besides those already stated above, here are a few more that guided Bonhoeffer all his life.

1. "Being a Christian is less about cautiously avoiding sin than about courageously and actively doing God's will: 'The essence of chastity is not the suppression of lust, but the total orientation of one's life towards a goal. Without such goal, chastity is bound to become ridiculous…'"[21]

2. "I discovered later… that it is only by living completely in this world that one learns to have faith… By this – worldliness I mean living unreservedly in life's duties, problems, successes and failures, experiences and perplexities. In so doing we throw ourselves completely into the arms of God, taking seriously not our own sufferings, but those of God in the world-watching with Christ in Gethsemane. That, I think, is faith…"[22]

3. "Christians who venture to stand on earth on only one leg will stand in heaven on only one leg too."[23]

4. "We know not what to do; but our eyes are upon Thee."[24]

5. "Only the believer is obedient, and only he who obeys believes."[25] Jesus said it this way, "If anyone loves me, he will obey my teaching" (John 14:23).

Dietrich Bonhoeffer's impact is difficult to quantify, but Bonhoeffer recognized that there was only One who could properly quantify his metrics. Much more was written about him after his death than during his time on earth. He has surely touched tens of millions of lives because he lived his life fruitfully for Christ. Being like Christ was his goal, and obedience to the Father was the other central goal of his life. He depended on hearing from God to guide him on his final mission, and although his family was central to his life, his love for God and others drove him to make the ultimate sacrifice. Without a doubt, God would say Dietrich became like Christ in his death: he followed Jesus.

One of Bonhoeffer's concepts relates to Roman 8:28, which is the main underlying theme for this book. In Chapter Five of his book, Metaxas writes about Bonhoeffer's decision-making process and the self-consciousness he brought to it.

"'I myself find the way such a decision comes about to be problematic. One thing is clear to me… that one personally—that is, consciously—has very little control over the ultimate yes or no, but rather that time decides everything. Recently I have noticed again and again that all the decisions I had to make were not really my own decisions. Whenever there was a dilemma, I just left it in abeyance and—without really consciously dealing with it intensively—let it grow toward the clarity of a decision. But this clarity is not so much intellectual as it is instinctive. The decision is made; whether one can adequately justify it retrospectively is another question. Thus it happened that I went.'"

I believe Bonhoeffer recognized that God caused things to work out according to His plan. Bonhoeffer's sole desire was to be used by God to do God's will. He wanted what God wanted so it was easy to be moved along by God. For me, I find myself "kicking against the goads" (Acts 26:14), planting my feet in the mud, and not wanting to be guided by the circumstances that God has sent to move me. I take a long time to recognize what God wants.

Bonhoeffer realized that even in tough situations, which not many of us will ever experience, God's hand was involved, and God was guiding him.

Solomon wrote the following concerning our plans and God's guidance. "In his heart a man plans his course, but the Lord determines his steps" (Proverbs 16:9).

My prayer is that as I move through life, I can completely embrace the idea that "God causes everything to work together for… good… For God knew his people in advance, and he chose them to become like his Son…" (Romans 8:28-29, NLT). I want to embrace these verses even if things do not look good, even if there is pain, and even if the impact is costly at the moment.

I know for myself, I am far away from becoming like Christ so it is a good thing that I can take this journey with you. As we walk, I pray that we will thrive through the disasters that may lie ahead.

THRIVING BY FINDING YOUR CAUSE: BECOME LIKE JESUS

Matthew Barnett wrote a splendid book *The Cause Within You* in which he talks about a God-given cause that each one of us has. His proud dad, Tommy Barnett writes in the foreword, "…everybody must have a cause if they're going to be happy in life." All great men of God found their causes for their lives. Not all causes are monumental, but God designed you for your cause.

Joseph of Arimathea asked Pilate for the body of Christ after His crucifixion, and he and Nicodemus prepared Jesus for burial. "With him came Nicodemus, the man who had come to Jesus at night. He brought seventy-five pounds of perfumed ointment made from myrrh and aloes. Following Jewish burial custom, they wrapped Jesus' body with the spices in long sheets of linen cloth" (John 19:39-40, NLT). Could this have been the great cause in their life? Can you imagine preparing the mangled, bloody body of Jesus for burial and applying seventy-five pounds of myrrh and aloes along with strips of cloth? On that night, no one was around, no one knew what was happening, and they did not anticipate any special recognition from anyone. Preparing Jesus' body could not have been glorious, yet God was the Audience Who applauded.

God gave Bonhoeffer a cause, which was religious freedom for the Jews and also for the Christians in Germany. If the German church would not stand up for the Jews, Christianity in Germany would die a slow death. He might not have been personally close to any Jew or had any special concern or care for them, but he knew God cared so he risked his life and eventually was hanged for his cause.

God has a cause for each of us. Our cause is commensurate with how much God entrusts to us. Greater causes require more of God's hand to complete the cause and greater faith. He gives us resources, gifts, and talents, yet He does not want us to depend on them to complete the work. We can do smaller things, but not eternal things. Greater causes require God to move. Bonhoeffer had great resources, gifts, and talents, but those were only starters. He needed faith from God to run the race and finish his work. God did now show up and break him out of Flossenburg prison at the last minute like He did with Apostles Peter and Paul. Bonhoeffer was hung. What did Bonhoeffer accomplish through his hanging? His faith was tested and he earned a perfect score.

Bonhoeffer's cause had something in common with the great men and women of God. His cause was for others. He was willing to give his life for the God-given cause. Most of us might not be willing to give our lives for the cause today, but maybe one day? For me, maybe a much smaller target might help me get there. Instead of giving my life, maybe I can shoot for giving all I have. Maybe I can start with something more than just my tithe. Maybe God allows us to grow into this greater call so that our faith grows proportionately. Maybe He knows we are wretched, and we love what we love. We hang on to what we value, including good things, such as family. If Bonhoeffer did that, he would have clung to his fiancée Maria and not joined the resistance.

Bonhoeffer had something from Jesus that I know I am lacking. He trusted God completely, and because of that trust, his faith grew. He could have stayed in New York, become a renowned professor, married Maria, and had many children. That would have been my choice. But then, what would his cause have been? Instead, because he knew God's mission for him, he trusted God, and his faith grew daily. Maybe becoming like Jesus requires trusting God like Jesus, "Yet not my will, but yours be done" (Matthew 26:39).

In my Christian walk, God had to "trick" me into moving forward because, like Peter, I want what I want, and I am slow to see God's hand guiding me. As He led me to salvation at First Assembly of God, to teaching, to ministering with the Salvation Army, Teen Challenge, and Surfing the Nations, to pastoring at Hawaii Cedar Church/Cedar Assembly of God, I did not move forward with gusto. My walk was usually a slow but constant walk with God. The good thing for me is God is patient.

FAITH HELPS US BECOME LIKE JESUS

The one thing I have learned about living for a cause that will help me become like Jesus and help me thrive even in an economic disaster is the cause has to be for others, not myself. I think for most of my life, I mostly thought about myself, even in ministry. I always thought God was causing all things to work together for my good, but a major thought arose for me as I was writing this book, "What if God was causing all things to work together for others' good?"

What if God wants believers to see things in that light? When anything happens in my life, whether good or bad for me, what if God desired that my heart's desire would be to come alongside Jesus to help Him work things out for other peoples' good? What, me help Jesus?

What if I really believed that any painful event in the lives of my family, extended family, friends, church members, atheists, and even enemies, was not a humbug for me but that God was working for their good? What if He was using my momentary interaction with them to work things so they too could become like Jesus? God would do the work, but He wanted to use my hands. Wouldn't that be great?

Jesus asks a question in the parable of the persistent widow. "However, when the Son of Man comes, will he find faith on the earth?" (Luke 18:8). Jesus is asking us if we can walk through life, experience trials, pray to Him, and not receive the answer we desire, but keep praying and trust Him? If we can, He would say, "Father, I have found faith on earth."

Life is not fair, but God will eventually make it fair later. If Jesus was speaking Hawaiian pidgin, he would say, "Try wait." If we trust Him, we can wait.

Our cause helps us to keep walking because we know God assigned our cause to us. Staying connected with family or a group of believers who will stand with us will help us get to the place of trusting in God. When two or three gather in His name, Jesus joins the group. He is helping us become like Him. Slowly our faith will grow. If we want to become like Jesus, we must have people standing by us, and we must be standing with them no matter what happens, praying for each other, praying for God's kingdom to come to earth, trusting each other, believing together, and having faith that God will answer and deliver us in His time. Growing together in faith is why family is so important, whether blood family or hani family.

My prayer for you is that you find your cause, something for which you are willing to die and give your all. God will use your cause to help you become like Jesus and become fruitful in your life, family, ministry, and workplace. You will thrive no matter the circumstances or disasters that unfold. Thriving no matter what would be the COOLEST ☺.

NOTES

INTRODUCTION

1. "thrive," *Merriam-Webster Online Dictionary*, accessed May 10, 2014. http://www.merriam-webster.com/dictionary/thrive.

CHAPTER 1

1. Eric Metaxas, *Bonhoeffer: Pastor, Martyr, Prophet, Spy* (Nashville: Thomas Nelson, 2010), 539.

2. Ben S. Bernanke, "Deflation: Making Sure 'It' Doesn't Happen Here" (remarks, National Economists Club, Washington, D.C., November 21, 2002).

3. John Mauldin, "Economic Singularity," *Thoughts from the Frontline*, October 15, 2012. https://www.mauldineconomics.com/frontlinethoughts/economic-singularity.

CHAPTER 3

1. Dannah Gresh, *Six Ways to Keep the "Good" in Your Boy* (Eugene: Harvest House, 2012), e-book, 1104.

CHAPTER 6

1. "Keynesian economics," *Wikipedia, the Free Encyclopedia*, accessed May 11, 2014. http://en.wikipedia.org/wiki/Keynesian_economics.

2. "Austrian business cycle theory," *Wikipedia, the Free Encyclopedia*, accessed May 11, 2014. http://en.wikipedia.org/wiki/Austrian_business_cycle_theory.

3. http://www.treasurydirect.gov/govt/reports/pd/histdebt/histdebt.htm accessed September 2, 2014.

4. http://www.bea.gov Table 1.1.5 Gross Domestic Product, accessed September 2, 2014.

5. Nassim Nicholas Taleb, *The Black Swan: The Impact of the Highly Improbable* (New York: Random House, 2007), e-book, 369.

6. Ibid, 400.

7. Ibid, 433.

8. Ibid, 453.

9. Ibid, 737.

10. "ubiquity," *Merriam-Webster Online Dictionary*, accessed May 18, 2014. http://www.merriam-webster.com/dictionary/ubiquity.

11. Mark Buchanan, *Ubiquity: Why Catastrophes Happen* (New York: Crown, 2000), e-book, 16.

12. Ibid.

13. Ibid, 2-3.

14. Ibid, 228.

15. Ibid, 234.

16. Ibid, 16.

17. John Mauldin, "Economic Singularity," *Thoughts from the Frontline*, October 15, 2012. https://www.mauldineconomics.com/frontlinethoughts/economic-singularity.

18. Matt Redman, "Blessed Be Your Name," *Blessed Be Your Name: The Songs of Matt Redman Vol. 1*, 2005, Survivor Records.

19. Ray Pensador, "Why 'High-Functioning' Psychopaths Rule the World," *Daily Kos*, September 10, 2011. http://www.dailykos.com/story/2011/09/10/1015320/-Why-High-Functioning-Psychopaths-Rule-The-World#.

20. Ibid.

21. Ibid.

22. Mike Huckabee, interview with Neil Cavuto, *Fox News*, December 14, 2012. http://www.newsmax.com/TheWire/huckabee-god-clarifies-sandy-hook/2012/12/18/id/468163/.

23. Gary D. Halbert, "US Birth Rate Hits New Low – A Nation of Singles," *Outside the Box*, December 18, 2012. https://www.mauldineconomics.com/outsidethebox/us-birth-rate-hits-new-low-a-nation-of-singles.

24. Central Intelligence Agency, World Factbook, World Fertility Rates, 2011

25. George Friedman, *The Next 100 Years: A Forecast for the 21ˢᵗ Century* (New York: Doubleday, 2009), 40.

26. J. Vernon McGee, *Through the Bible* (Nashville: Thomas Nelson, 1981), 54.

27. "Bretton Woods system," *Wikipedia, the Free Encyclopedia*, accessed July 20, 2014. http://en.wikipedia.org/wiki/Bretton_Woods_system.

28. Ibid.

CHAPTER 7

1. Malcolm Gladwell, *The Tipping Point: How Little Things Can Make a Big Difference* (New York: Little, Brown and Company, 2000), 140-141.

2. Ibid, 152-154.

3. Ed Silvoso, *That None Should Perish: How to Reach Entire Cities for Christ through Prayer Evangelism* (Regal Books: Ventura, 1994), e-book, 970.

4. Eric Metaxas, *Bonhoeffer: Pastor, Martyr, Prophet, Spy* (Nashville: Thomas Nelson, 2010), 5.

5. Ibid, 6-7.

6. Ibid.

7. Ibid, 41.

8. Ibid, 37.

9. Ibid, 329.

10. Ibid, 335.

11. Ibid.

12. Ibid, 359-360.

13. Ibid.

14. Ibid, 361.

15. Ibid, 530-531.

16. Ibid.

17. Ibid.

18. Ibid.

19. Ibid.

20. Ibid.

21. Ibid, 485.

22. Ibid, 484.

23. Ibid, 456.

24. Ibid, 540.

25. Ibid.

OTHER BOOKS BY JIMMY YAMADA

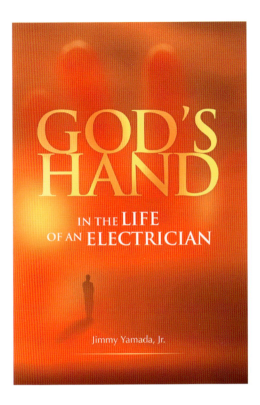

GOD'S HAND IN THE LIFE OF AN ELECTRICIAN (2008)

A great gift is to see God's hand on your life. In this life memoir, Jimmy Yamada, Jr. – a prominent Hawai'i businessman and ministry leader – looks back at the jagged shards of his past to see a clear pattern of God's design. And like sun streaming through a stained-glass cathedral, God truly makes all things good in His time. If God can do this for Jimmy Yamada, Jr., He can surely do it for you!

WHITE
MOUNTAIN
CASTLE
PUBLISHING, LLC

www.whitemountaincastle.com